# THE REPUBLIC

*Plato*

EDITORIAL DIRECTOR Justin Kestler
EXECUTIVE EDITOR Ben Florman
DIRECTOR OF TECHNOLOGY Tammy Hepps

SERIES EDITORS Boomie Aglietti, John Crowther, Justin Kestler
MANAGING EDITOR Vince Janoski

WRITER Yael Goldstein
EDITORS Jesse Hawkes, Lawrence Gaccon Gladney

This edition published by Spark Publishing

Spark Publishing
A Division of SparkNotes LLC
120 Fifth Avenue, 8th Floor
New York, NY 10011

Please submit all comments and questions or report errors to www.sparknotes.com/errors

Library of Congress Catalog-in-Publication Data available upon request

Printed in China

ISBN 1-58663-375-9

# INTRODUCTION: STOPPING TO BUY SPARKNOTES ON A SNOWY EVENING

Whose words these are you *think* you know.
Your paper's due tomorrow, though;
We're glad to see you stopping here
To get some help before you go.

Lost your course? You'll find it here.
Face tests and essays without fear.
Between the words, good grades at stake:
Get great results throughout the year.

Once school bells caused your heart to quake
As teachers circled each mistake.
Use SparkNotes and no longer weep,
Ace every single test you take.

Yes, books are lovely, dark, and deep,
But only what you grasp you keep,
With hours to go before you sleep,
With hours to go before you sleep.

# CONTENTS

# CONTEXT

## PLATO'S LIFE

Plato was born in Athens in 428 B.C. to an aristocratic family. Ancient sources claim that his father, Ariston, was a descendant of Codrus, the last king of Athens, and his mother, Perictione, of Solon, an almost mythical Athenian lawgiver and the author of the city's first constitution. Plato's two brothers, Glaucon and Adeimantus, appear as two of the main characters in the *Republic*.

Ariston died during Plato's boyhood, and Perictione remarried Pyrilampes, a friend of the Athenian statesman Pericles. With his noble birth and intellectual talents, young Plato had fine prospects in Athenian politics. The political upheavals of his youth attracted him to the public sphere.

Two major upheavals turned Plato away from politics. The first was the assumption of power by two groups—the Four Hundred and the Thirty. These factions of wealthy citizens seized control at the end of the Peloponnesian War and turned Athens into an oligarchy. Plato had mixed feelings about the takeover. He was related to Charmides, a member of the Thirty. But his nascent rational outlook made him critical of the government for its tyrannical leanings and instability. He was active in supporting the restoration of democracy, but that system proved itself less than perfectly just in 399 B.C. In that year, Plato's mentor, Socrates, an eccentric philosopher and a cult figure among the Athenian youth, stood before a jury of about 500 Athenians on charges of not recognizing the gods of the state, of inventing new deities, and of corrupting the youth of Athens. More than these charges, Socrates' close association with a number of men who had fallen out of political favor in Athens brought him to trial. Because an amnesty had been declared for political offenders, other charges had to be brought against him. Socrates was found guilty by a narrow margin and sentenced to death.

After Socrates' death, Plato devoted himself to continuing the work of his teacher. He spent years traveling around the Mediterranean, teaching and learning. Among the places he visited was Sicily, the center of Pythagorean thought. In 387 B.C., Plato resettled in Athens and founded the Academy, probably the first institution of its kind, and the model for the Western university. Plato and other teachers instructed students from all over the Mediterranean in metaphysics, epistemology, ethics, politics, and the natural and mathematical sciences. Although the Academy was not meant to prepare students for any sort of profession, such as politics, law, or medicine, the topics taught there were not divorced from the larger world. Members of the Academy were invited by various cities to aid in the development of new constitutions. The Academy lasted in one form or another until A.D. 527, 912 years in total. Plato spent the rest of his life as the director of studies at the Academy, although it is not at all clear that he himself taught there. He is thought to have written the *Republic* there in around 380 B.C. The most famous student of the Academy during this time was the philosopher Aristotle.

From 385 B.C. until his death in 347, Plato only left the Academy twice, both times to visit Sicily. What drew him away from his school was the possibility of putting the political theory he outlined in the *Republic* into practice. In 367 B.C., Dionysus I, tyrant of Sicily, died. His brother Dion, father of the heir, had been a student of Plato's and immediately sent for his teacher. Unfortunately, Dionysus II remained unconvinced that the vigorous study of mathematics and philosophy would be the best preparation for his rule, and so the world lost its chance to test the first philosopher-king.

## HISTORICAL CONTEXT

Philosophy first emerged in the sixth century B.C. on the Greek island of Miletus. The first philosophers focused on questions of natural science, trying to explain the world that they observed around them in terms of a few simple principles. Little attention was given to issues in ethics and politics. Poets, not the philosophers addressed the values of the society. Poets like Hesiod and Homer outlined the virtues that marked the good Greek man. They found motivation for good behavior in the promise of divine reward.

In the fifth century B.C., two tremendous political upheavals cast traditional Greek values into question and thrust issues of ethics into the hands of the philosophers. From 431 to 404 Athens and Sparta were engaged in the Peloponnesian War, which Athens finally lost. The ravages of war cast doubt on the martial virtues of Homeric heroes, and the growth of democracies, especially in Athens, called for new civic virtue: the ability to speak persuasively in the assemblies and law courts became more valuable than warcraft.

In this Athenian climate a new class emerged: the Sophists, itinerant teachers who would offer instruction in nearly any subject if the student was willing and able to pay a fee. Their focus was on rhetorical skills, and they emphasized the primacy of persuasiveness over truth. The Sophists exploited the new uncertainty about traditional moral values. There was no cohesive school of Sophism, and the views of teachers varied widely. What we know of their thought indicates that they frequently claimed that whether or not an action is right or wrong is less important than whether or not it benefits the interests of the agent. Many argued that there were no such things as right and wrong—that objective moral standards did not exist. Some denied any possibility of objective truth and scoffed at the idea of objective knowledge. They claimed that morality is a convention imposed by the rulers of societies upon their subjects. In the *Republic*, the Sophist Thrasymachus declares that immorality is a virtue because it enables us to advance in the competition of life. In Plato's dialogue the *Gorgias*, an even stronger view is attributed to a man named Callicles; he claims that conventional morality is unjust because it attempts to deprive the strong of their natural right to exploit the weak. While some Sophists, such as Hippias, were adamant in their refusal of such doctrines, we have reason to believe that the trend toward a belief in justice as the interest of the stronger was strong among Sophists.

In this moral climate, Soctrates was motivated by a desire to combat what he viewed as forces creeping against morality. Socrates was disturbed by what he perceived to be the moral complacency of the Athenian citizens; he watched with concern as they lived their lives in a selfish, unreflective haze, focusing on gaining and increasing their own power and using the theories of the Sophists to justify their attitude. His solution was to act as a "gadfly," stinging his fellow citizens into moral self-examination. He stood in the marketplace daily, trying to engage anyone he could in conversation. The unexamined life, he declared, was not worth living, and so he would force everyone he encountered to reflect on their lives, their beliefs, and their motivations.

Plato took over this mission when Socrates died. He too wanted to combat immorality and selfishness, which were still widespread. He also wanted to combat the Sophists' other skeptical claims: their avowal that there is no such thing as objective truth, no possibility of objective knowledge.

# PHILOSOPHICAL CONTEXT

Plato's dialogues are classed into early, middle, and late periods. The early dialogues, written soon after Socrates' death, provide the nearest portrayal of what Socrates' philosophy might have been. In these dialogues, Plato focuses almost exclusively on ethical questions, using the Socratic method of *elenchus*. In a typical early dialogue, Socrates asks his interlocuter for a definition of some virtue (piety, courage, etc.); once the definition is offered, he shows that the definition is inconsistent with other beliefs that the interlocuter holds. The interlocuter refines his definition, and Socrates shows that the new version is still inconsistent with other beliefs. This cycle of revisions and rebuttals is intended to continue until a satisfactory definition is reached, but this never actually happens in any of the dialogues. With the exception of a few key doctrines, no idea ever emerges from *elenchus* still looking tenable. A typical early dialogue ends in a state of *aporia*—intellectual gridlock, where all existing beliefs on the topic have been rebutted, but progress seems impossible. The interlocuters know what they thought before was wrong, but they are not told what to believe instead.

These dialogues should not be considered failures. According to Socrates, the goal of *elenchus* is not to reach definitions. He claimed that engaging in philosophic dialectic is crucial to human well-being—rendering people both happier and more virtuous. He believed this so strongly that, by some accounts, he chose to be executed rather than give up the practice. Though in the early dialogues Plato utilizes Socratic methods, he does not accept everything taught to him by Socrates. He explores many of these views critically, laying them out but not necessarily endorsing them.

In the middle period, Plato develops a distinct voice and philosophical outlook. The figure of Socrates becomes more of a mouthpiece for Plato's own views. He relies less on the method of *elenchus* and presents his dialogues as conversation between a teacher and his students rather than as debate between a philosopher and his opponents. Instead of *aporia*, interlocuters arrice at positive conclusions. Ideas hinted at in the early dialogues, such as the theory of Forms, emerge as full-fledged doctrines. Plato's interests broaden beyond ethics into epistemology and metaphysics. He draws on his theory of Forms and the idea of the soul to explore old questions about how to live, the nature and role of love, and the nature of the physical world.

The theory of Forms grounds most of the other theory Plato puts forward in his middle period. It is also his response to the challenge of the Sophists and their claim that there is no objective truth, moral or otherwise. The theory of Forms proposes that in addition to the physical world we sense around us, there is another realm of reality. This realm, a purely intelligible rather than observable sphere of existence, is made up of eternal, absolute, unchanging, perfect Forms which define all that exists fleetingly and imperfectly in the world of our senses. The Forms provide knowledge of objective truth.

The *Republic* is paradigmatic of the shift from the early to middle periods. Book I adheres to the structure of a typical early dialogue. Some speculate that it originally stood on its own as a dialogue dating from the early period (in which case it would have been called *Thrasymachus*). Plato has Socrates use the method of *elenchus* in an attempt to pry out a definition of justice, and the result is *aporia*. Instead of leaving off there, Socrates picks up the question in Book II. He hashes out a detailed positive theory of justice over the course of nine more books. In these books, rather than employing the *elenchus,* Socrates mostly lectures, pausing intermittently to respond to objections raised by his students, Plato's two brothers. In Book VII, Socrates warns against *elenchus*. He declares that philosophical dialectic is dangerous in the wrong hands and should only be taught to the right people and only then when they are old enough to use it properly. He warns that those without the proper respect for truth would use the method in order to argue against everything instead of using it to seek out what is right. This discussion might explain what motivated Plato's shift in methods of inquiry and what motivated him to found the Academy.

The later dialogues are extremely difficult and controversial. They contain Plato's most complex philosophical and logical views, and there is little agreement over what trends and themes define this period. One work among this later group is worth mentioning in relation to the *Republic*. In the *Laws,* possibly Plato's last work, he constructs another ideal state. Though this state too is authoritarian, it has democratic elements and differs vastly from the state portrayed in the *Republic*. Plato grew more willing to compromise principles in order to find something that might work in practice. He came to emphasize the value of the rule of law, whereas in the *Republic* he suggested that law was unnecessary in a city with the right rulers.

# OVERVIEW

WHY DO MEN BEHAVE JUSTLY? Is it because they fear societal punishment? Are they trembling before notions of divine retribution? Do the stronger elements of society scare the weak into submission in the name of law? Or do men behave justly because it is good for them to do so? Is justice, regardless of its rewards and punishments, a good thing in and of itself? How do we define justice? Plato sets out to answer these questions in the *Republic*. He wants to define justice, and to define it in such a way as to show that justice is worthwhile in and of itself. He meets these two challenges with a single solution: a definition of justice that appeals to human psychology, rather than to perceived behavior.

Plato's strategy in the *Republic* is to first explicate the primary notion of societal, or political, justice, and then to derive an analogous concept of individual justice. In Books II, III, and IV, Plato identifies political justice as harmony in a structured political body. An ideal society consists of three main classes of people—producers (craftsmen, farmers, artisans, etc.), auxiliaries (warriors), and guardians (rulers); a society is just when relations between these three classes are right. Each group must perform its appropriate function, and only that function, and each must be in the right position of power in relation to the others. Rulers must rule, auxiliaries must uphold rulers' convictions, and producers must limit themselves to exercising whatever skills nature granted them (farming, blacksmithing, painting, etc.) Justice is a principle of specialization: a principle that requires that each person fulfill the societal role to which nature fitted him and not interfere in any other business.

At the end of Book IV, Plato tries to show that individual justice mirrors political justice. He claims that the soul of every individual has a three part structure analagous to the three classes of a society. There is a rational part of the soul, which seeks after truth and is responsible for our philosophical inclinations; a spirited part of the soul, which desires honor and is responsible for our feelings of anger and indignation; and an appetitive part of the soul, which lusts after all sorts of things, but money most of all (since money must be used to fulfill any other base desire). The just individual can be defined in analogy with the just society; the three parts of his soul achieve the requisite relationships of power and influence in regard to one another. In a just individual, the rational part of the soul rules, the spirited part of the soul supports this rule, and the appetitive part of the soul submits and follows wherever reason leads. Put more plainly: in a just individual, the entire soul aims at fulfilling the desires of the rational part, much as in the just society the entire community aims at fulfilling whatever the rulers will.

The parallels between the just society and the just individual run deep. Each of the three classes of society, in fact, is dominated by one of the three parts of the soul. Producers are dominated by their appetites—their urges for money, luxury, and pleasure. Warriors are dominated by their spirits, which make them courageous. Rulers are dominated by their rational faculties and strive for wisdom. Books V through VII focus on the rulers as the philosopher kings.

In a series of three analogies—the allegories of the sun, the line, and the cave—Plato explains who these individuals are while hammering out his theory of the Forms. Plato explains that the world is divided into two realms, the visible (which we grasp with our senses) and the intelligible (which we only grasp with our mind). The visible world is the universe we see around us. The intelligible world is comprised of the Forms—abstract, changeless absolutes such as Goodness, Beauty, Redness, and Sweetness that exist in permanent relation to the visible realm and make it possible. (An apple is red and sweet, the theory goes, because it participates in the Forms of Redness and Sweetness.) Only the Forms are objects of knowledge, because only they possess the eternal unchanging truth that the mind—not the senses—must apprehend.

Only those whose minds are trained to grasp the Forms—the philosophers—can know anything at all. In particular, what the philosophers must know in order to become able rulers is the Form of the Good—the source of all other Forms, and of knowledge, truth, and beauty. Plato cannot describe this Form directly, but he claims that it is to the intelligible realm what the sun is to the visible realm. Using the allegory of the cave, Plato paints an evocative portrait of the philosopher's soul moving through various stages of cognition (represented by the line) through the visible realm into the intelligible, and finally grasping the Form of the Good. The aim of education is not to put knowledge into the soul, but to put the right desires into the soul—to fill the soul with a lust for truth, so that it desires to move past the visible world, into the intelligible, ultimately to the Form of the Good.

Philosophers form the only class of men to possess knowledge and are also the most just men. Their souls, more than others, aim to fulfil the desires of the rational part. After comparing the philosopher king to the most unjust type of man—represented by the tyrant, who is ruled entirely by his non-rational appetites—Plato claims that justice is worthwhile for its own sake. In Book IX he presents three arguments for the conclusion that it is desirable to be just. By sketching a psychological portrait of the tyrant, he attempts to prove that injustice tortures a man's psyche, whereas a just soul is a healthy, happy one, untroubled and calm. Next he argues that, though each of the three main character types—money-loving, honor-loving, and truth-loving—have their own conceptions of pleasure and of the corresponding good life—each choosing his own life as the most pleasant—only the philosopher can judge because only he has experienced all three types of pleasure. The others should accept the philosopher's judgement and conclude that the pleasures associated with the philosophical are most pleasant and thus that the just life is also most pleasant. He tries to demonstrate that only philosophical pleasure is really pleasure at all; all other pleasure is nothing more than cessation of pain.

One might notice that none of these arguments actually prove that justice is desirable apart from its consequences—instead, they establish that justice is always accompanied by true pleasure. In all probability, none of these is actually supposed to serve as the main reason why justice is desirable. Instead, the desirability of justice is likely connected to the intimate relationship between the just life and the Forms. The just life is good in and of itself because it involves grasping these ultimate goods, and imitating their order and harmony, thus incorporating them into one's own life. Justice is good, in other words, because it is connected to the greatest good, the Form of the Good.

Plato ends the *Republic* on a surprising note. Having defined justice and established it as the greatest good, he banishes poets from his city. Poets, he claims, appeal to the basest part of the soul by imitating unjust inclinations. By encouraging us to indulge ignoble emotions in sympathy with the characters we hear about, poetry encourages us to indulge these emotions in life. Poetry, in sum, makes us unjust. In closing, Plato relates the myth of Er, which describes the trajectory of a soul after death. Just souls are rewarded for one thousand lifetimes, while unjust ones are punished for the same amount of time. Each soul then must choose its next life.

# IMPORTANT TERMS

*Aporia*    Aporia is the Greek term for the state of helplessness—the inability to proceed—that ends all of Plato's early dialogues. Through his pointed questioning, Socrates succeeds in showing that his interlocuters have no appropriate definition for the topic under consideration (be that topic piety, love, courage, justice, or whatever else), but nor is he able to supply one himself. In Book I of the Republic Socrates brings his friends to a state of aporia on the topic of justice, but then in the next nine books he manages to move beyond the aporia and give an actual answer to the question at hand.

*Appetite*    Appetite is the largest aspect of our tripartite soul. It is the seat of all our various desires for food, drink, sexual gratification and other such pleasures. It contains both necessary desires, which should be indulged (such as the desire to eat enough to stay alive), unnecessary desires, which should be limited (such as the desire to eat a ten pound sirloin steak at every meal), and unlawful desires, which should be suppressed at all costs (such as the desire to eat one's children). Though the appetite lusts after many things, Plato dubs it "money-loving," since money is required for satisfying most of these desires. In a just man, the appetite is strictly controlled by reason and reason's henchman, spirit.

*Auxiliary*    Plato divides his just society into three classes: the producers, the auxiliaries, and the guardians. The auxiliaries are the warriors, responsible for defending the city from invaders, and for keeping the peace at home. They must enforce the convictions of the guardians, and ensure that the producers obey.

Belief     Belief is the second lowest grade of cognitive activity. The object of belief is the visible realm rather than the intelligible realm. A man in a state of belief does not have any access to the Forms, but instead takes sensible particulars as the most real things.

Elenchus     Elenchus is the Greek term for Socrates' method of questioning his interlocuters. In an elenchus he attempts to show that their own beliefs are contradictory, and thus to prove that they do not have knowledge about some topic about which they thought they had knowledge.

Empirical     When something is an empirical question, that means that the question can only be settled by going out into the world and investigating. The question, "What percentage of the population of the United States likes ice cream" is an example of an empirical question, which can only be answered through empirical investigation. The question "What is the square root of two," on the other hand, is not an empirical question. In order to answer this question all you have to do is think about the mathematics involved; you do not have investigate evidence in the world.

Epistemology     The branch of philosophy concerned with knowledge, belief, and thought. Epistemological questions include: What is knowledge? How do we form beliefs based on evidence? Can we know anything?

Form     According to Plato's metaphysical theory, there is an aspect of reality beyond the one which we can see, an aspect of reality even more real than the one we see. This aspect of reality, the intelligible realm, is comprised of unchanging, eternal, absolute entities, which are called "Forms." These absolute entities— such as Goodness, Beauty, Redness, Sourness, and so on—are the cause of all the objects we experience around us in the visible realm. An apple is red and sweet, for instance, because it participates in the Form of Redness and the Form of Sweetness. A woman is beautiful because she participates in the Form of Beauty. Only the Forms can be objects of knowledge (that is, Forms are the only things we can know about).

*Form of the Good*  Among the Forms, one stands out as most important. This is the Form of the Good. Plato is unable to tell us exactly what the Form of The Good is, but he does tell us that it is the source of intelligibility and of our capacity to know, and also that it is responsible for bringing all of the other Forms into existence. He compares its role in the intelligible realm to the role of the sun in the visible realm. The Form of the Good is the ultimate object of knowledge; it is only once one grasps the Form of the Good that one reaches the highest grade of cognitive activity, understanding. Therefore, it is only after he grasps the Form of the Good that a philosopher-in-training becomes a philosopher-king.

*Guardian*  Plato divides his just society into three classes: the producers, the auxiliaries, and the guardians. The guardians are responsible for ruling the city. They are chosen from among the ranks of the auxiliaries, and are also known as philosopher-kings.

*Hesiod*  Hesiod was a famous Greek poet. His long poem Works and Days outlines the traditional Greek conception of virtue and justice.

*Imagination*  Imagination is the lowest grade of cognitive activity. Someone in the state of imagination takes mere images and shadows as the most real things. Probably, this means that such a person derives his ideas about himself and the world from products of art, such as poetry in Plato's day and movies and television in our own. See also Belief, Thought, Understanding.

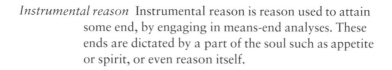

*Instrumental reason*  Instrumental reason is reason used to attain some end, by engaging in means-end analyses. These ends are dictated by a part of the soul such as appetite or spirit, or even reason itself.

*Intelligible realm*  Plato divides all of existence up into two parts: the visible realm and the intelligible realm. The intelligible realm cannot be sensed, but only grasped with the intellect. It consists of the Forms. Only the intelligible realm can be the object of knowledge.

*Kallipolis*  Kallipolis is the Greek term for Plato's just city.

*Knowledge*  According to Plato, knowledge can only pertain to eternal, unchanging truths. I can know, for instance that two plus two equals four, because this will also be the case. I cannot know, however, that Meno is beautiful. For this reason, only the intelligible realm, the realm of the Forms can be the object of knowledge. See also Opinion.

*Lover of sights and sounds*  "Lovers of sights and sounds" is Socrates' term for the pseudo-intellectuals who claim to have expertise regarding all that is beautiful, but who fail to recognize that there is such a thing as the Form of the Beautiful, which causes all beauty in the visible realm. Socrates is adamant that lovers of sights and sounds be distinguished from philosophers, who grasp the Forms, and thus have knowledge. Lovers of sights and sounds have no knowledge, only opinion.

*Metaphysics*  The branch of philosophy concerned with asking what there is in the world. The theory of Forms is a metaphysical theory, as is the theory of the tripartite soul.

*Opinion*  Since only eternal, unchanging truths can be the objects of knowledge, all other truths are relegated to opinion. Opinion is the highest form of certainty that we can hope for when it comes to the visible realm, the realm of sensible particulars.

*Philosopher-king*  The philosopher-king is the ruler of the kallipolis. Also called guardians, philosopher-kings are the only people who can grasp the Forms, and thus the only people who can claim actual knowledge. Since the philosopher-king yearns after truth above all else, he is also the most just man.

*Pleonexia*  A Greek term meaning "the desire to have more," pleonexia refers to the yearning after money and power. In Book I, Thrasymachus presents the popular view that justice is nothing more than an unnatural restraint on our natural pleonexia.

*Producers*  Plato divides his just society into three classes: the producers, the auxiliaries, and the guardians. The producing class is the largest class of society; it is a catch-all group that includes all professions other than warrior and ruler. Framers and craftsmen are producers, as are merchants, doctors, artists, actors, lawyers, judges, and so forth. In a just society, the producers have no share in ruling, but merely obey what the rulers decree. They focus exclusively on producing whatever it is that they are best suited to produce (whether that be metal work, agriculture, shoes, or furniture).

*Reason*  Reason is one aspect of our tripartite soul. It lusts after truth and is the source of all of our philosophic desires. In the just man, the entire soul is ruled by reason, and strives to fulfill reason's desires. See also Appetite, Spirit.

*Sensible particular*  Sensible particulars are the objects that we experience all around us—trees, flowers, chairs—any physical objects. They are "sensible" because we can sense them with our sight, smell, hearing, taste, and touch; they are "particular," because they are particular items that undergo change over time, rather than universal, unchanging ideas. According to Plato's metaphysical picture, the visible realm is made up of sensible particulars. According to his epistemological picture, sensible particulars cannot be objects of knowledge but only of opinion.

*Sophist*  The Sophists were teachers-for-hire who educated the wealthy men of Athens in the fifth century B.C. Though they were a diverse group with diverse opinions, they tended to share a disregard for the notion of objective truth and knowledge. This disregard extended to the notion of objective moral truth, which means that they did not believe in such a things as "right" and "wrong." One of the guiding motivations in all of Plato's work was to prove the Sophists wrong: to show that there is such a thing as objective truth, and that we can have knowledge of this objective truth.

*Specialization*  The principle of specialization states that every man must fulfill the societal role to which nature best suits him, and should refrain from engaging in any other business. Those naturally suited to farm should farm, those naturally suited to heal should be doctors, those naturally suited to fight should be warriors, those naturally suited to be philosophers should rule, and so on. Plato believes that this simple rule is the guiding principle of society, and the source of political justice.

*Spirit*  Spirit is one aspect of our tripartite soul. It is the source of our honor-loving and victory-loving desires. Spirit is responsible for our feelings of anger and indignation. In a just soul, spirit acts as henchman to reason, ensuring that appetite adheres to reason's commands.

*Thought*    Thought is the second highest grade of cognitive activity. As with understanding, the objects of thought are the Forms of the intelligible realm. Unlike understanding, though, thought can only proceed with the crutches of images and hypotheses (i.e. unproven assumptions). See also Belief, Imagination, Understanding.

*Tripartite soul*  According to Plato, the human soul has three parts corresponding to the three classes of society in a just city. Individual justice consists in maintaining these three parts in the correct power relationships, which reason ruling, spirit aiding reason, and appetite obeying.

*Understanding*  Understanding is the highest grade of cognitive activity. Understanding involves the use of pure, abstract reason, and does not rely on the crutches of images and unproven assumptions. Understanding is only achieved once the Form of the Good is grasped. See also belief, imagination, thought.

*Visible realm*  Plato divides existence up into two realms, the visible realm and the intelligible realm. The visible realm can be grasped with our senses. It is comprised of the world see around us—the world of sensible particulars. The objects which comprise the visible realm are not as real as those which comprise the intelligible realm; in addition, they are not the proper objects of knowledge (i.e., we cannot "know" anything about them), but of opinion.

# PHILOSOPHICAL THEMES, ARGUMENTS & IDEAS

## JUSTICE AS THE ADVANTAGE OF THE STRONGER

In Book I of the *Republic*, Thrasymachus sets up a challenge to justice. Thrasymachus is a Sophist, one of the teachers-for-hire who preached a creed of subjective morality to the wealthy sons of Athens. The Sophists did not believe in objective truth, including objective moral truth. They did not think, in other words, that anything was absolutely "right" or "wrong"; instead they viewed all actions as either advantageous or disadvantageous to the person performing them. If an action was advantageous then they thought you should engage in it, and if it was disadvantageous then they thought that you should refrain. Taking this belief to its logical conclusion, some of them went so far as to claim that law and morality are nothing but mere convention, and that one ought to try to get away with injustice and illegality whenever such action would be to one's advantage. Plato meant to combat this attitude in the *Republic*.

Thrasymachus introduces the Sophist challenge by remarking that justice is nothing but the advantage of the stronger. He does not mean to define justice with this statement, but to debunk it. His claim proceeds from the basic Sophistic moral notion: that the norms considered just are nothing more than conventions which hamper those who adhere to them, and benefit those who flout them. Those who behave unjustly naturally gain power and become the rulers, the strong people in society. Justice is the advantage of the stronger because when stupid, weak people behave in accordance with justice, they are disadvantaged, and the strong (those who behave unjustly) are advantaged.

An alternate reading of Thrasymachus' bold statement makes his claim seem slightly more subtle. According to this reading (put forward by C.D.C. Reeve), Thrasymachus is not merely making the usual assertion that the norms of justice are conventions; he claims further that these mores and norms are conventions that were put in place by the rulers (the "stronger") for the purpose of promoting their own interests. Conceptions of justice, in this reading, are the products of propaganda and tools of oppressors.

Regardless of the interpretation we give to Thrasymachus' statement, the challenge to Socrates is the same: he must prove that justice is something good and desirable, that it is more than convention, that it is connected to objective standards of morality, and that it is in our interest to adhere to it. His attempt to meet this challenge occupies the rest of the *Republic*.

## THE PRINCIPLE OF SPECIALIZATION

Before he can prove that justice is a good thing, Plato must first state what justice is. Instead of defining justice as a set of behavioral norms (as the traditional Greek thinkers did) Plato identifies justice as structural: political justice resides in the structure of the city; individual justice resides in the structure of the soul. The just structure of the city is summed up by the principle of specialization: each member of society must play the role for which his nature best suits him and not meddle in any other business. A man whose nature suits him to farming must farm and do nothing else; a man whose nature best suits him to building objects out of wood must be a carpenter and not bother with any other sort of work. Plato believes that this is the only way to ensure that each job is done as well as possible.

The principle of specialization keeps the farmer from carpentering, and the carpenter from farming. More important, it keeps both the farmer and the carpenter from becoming warriors and rulers. The principle of specialization separates society into three classes: the class of producers (including farmers, craftsmen, doctors, etc.), the class of warriors, and the class of rulers. Specialization ensures that these classes remain in a fixed relations of power and influence. Rulers control the city, establishing its laws and objectives. Warriors carry out the commands of rulers. Producers stay out of political affairs, only worrying themselves about the business of ruling insofar as they need to obey what the rulers say and the warriors enforce. A city set up in this way, Plato contends, is a just city.

# THE TRIPARTITE SOUL

Just as political justice consists in the structural relations among classes of society, Plato believes, individual justice consists in correct structural relations among parts of the soul. Paralleling the producers, warriors, and rulers in the city, Plato claims that each individual soul has three separate seats of desire and motivation: the appetitive part of our soul lusts after food, drink, sex, and so on (and after money most of all, since money is the means of satisfying the rest of these desires); the spirited part of the soul yearns for honor; the rational part of the soul desires truth and knowledge. In a just soul, these three parts stand in the correct power relations. The rational part must rule, the spirited part must enforce the rational part's convictions, and the appetitive part must obey.

In the just soul, the desires of the rational, truth-loving part dictate the overall aims of the human being. All appetites and considerations of honor are put at the disposal of truth-loving goals. The just soul strives wholly toward truth. Plato identifies the philosopher (literally "truth lover") as the most just individual, and sets him up as ruler of the just city.

# THE SUN, THE LINE, THE CAVE

Explaining his idea of a philosopher-king, Plato appeals to three successive analogies to spell out the metaphysical and epistemological theories that account for the philosopher's irreplaceable role in politics. The analogy of the sun illuminates the notion of the Form of the Good, the philosopher-king's ultimate object of desire. The line illustrates the four different grades of cognitive activity of which a human being is capable, the highest of which only the philosopher-kings ever reach. The allegory of the cave demonstrates the effects of education on the human soul, demonstrating how we move from one grade of cognitive activity to the next.

In the allegory of the cave, Plato asks us to imagine the following scenario: A group of people have lived in a deep cave since birth, never seeing any daylight at all. These people are bound in such a way that they cannot look to either side or behind them, but only straight ahead. Behind them is a fire, and behind the fire is a partial wall. On top of the wall are various statues, which are manipulated by another group of people, laying out of sight. Because of the fire, the statues cast shadows on the wall that the prisoners are facing.

The prisoners watch the stories that these shadows play out, and because this is all they can ever see, they believe that these shadows are the most real things in the world. When they talk to one another about "men," "women," "trees," "horses," and so on, they refer only to these shadows.

Now he asks us to imagine that one of these prisoners is freed from his bonds, and is able to look at the fire and at the statues themselves. After initial pain and disbelief, he eventually realizes that all these things are more real than the shadows he has always believed to be the most real things; he grasps how the fire and the statues together caused the shadows, which are copies of the real things. He now takes the statues and fire as the most real things in the world.

Next this prisoner is dragged out of the cave into the world above. At first, he is so dazzled by the light in the open that he can only look at shadows, then he is able to look at reflections, then finally at the real objects—real trees, flowers, houses and other physical objects. He sees that these are even more real than the statues were, and that those objects were only copies of these.

Finally, when the prisoner's eyes have fully adjusted to the brightness, he lifts his sights toward the heavens and looks at the sun. He understands that the sun is the cause of everything he sees around him—of the light, of his capacity for sight, of the existence of flowers, trees, and all other objects.

The stages the prisoner passes through in the allegory of the cave correspond to the various levels on the line. The line, first of all, is broken into two equal halves: the visible realm (which we can grasp with our senses) and the intelligible realm (which we can only grasp with the mind). When the prisoner is in the cave he is in the visible realm. When he ascends into the daylight, he enters the intelligible.

The lowest rung on the cognitive line is imagination. In the cave, this is represented as the prisoner whose feet and head are bound, so that he can only see shadows. What he takes to be the most real things are not real at all; they are shadows, mere images. These shadows are meant to represent images from art. A man who is stuck in the imagination stage of development takes his truths from epic poetry and theater, or other fictions. He derives his conception of himself and his world from these art forms rather than from looking at the real world.

When the prisoner frees himself and looks at the statues he reaches the next stage in the line: belief. The statues are meant to correspond to the real objects of our sensation—real people, trees, flowers, and so on. The man in the cognitive stage of belief mistakenly takes these sensible particulars as the most real things.

When he ascends into the world above, though, he sees that there is something even more real: the Forms, of which the sensible particulars are imperfect copies. He is now at the stage of thought in his cognition. He can reason about Forms, but not in a purely abstract way. He uses images and unproven assumptions as crutches.

Finally, he turns his sights to the sun, which represents the ultimate Form, the Form of the Good. The Form of the Good is the cause of all other Forms, and is the source of all goodness, truth, and beauty in the world. It is the ultimate object of knowledge. Once the prisoner has grasped the Form of the Good, he has reached the highest stage of cognition: understanding. He no longer has any need for images or unproven assumptions to aid in his reasoning. By reaching the Form of the Good, he hits on the first principle of philosophy which explains everything without the need of any assumptions or images. He can now use this understanding derived from comprehending the Form of the Good to transform all his previous thought into understanding—he can understand all of the Forms. Only the philosopher can reach this stage, and that is why only he is fit to rule.

Plato is unable to provide direct detail about the Form of the Good, and instead illustrates his idea by comparing it to the sun. The Form of the Good is to the intelligible realm, he claims, as the sun is the visible realm. (In the metaphor, the fire in the cave represents the sun.) First of all, just as the sun provides light and visibility in the visible realm, the Form of the Good is the source of intelligibility. The sun makes sight possible, and, similarly, the Form of the Good is responsible for our capacity for knowledge. The sun causes things to come to be in the visible world; it regulates the seasons, makes flowers bloom, influences animals to give birth and so on. The Form of the Good is responsible for the existence of Forms, for their coming to be in the intelligible world.

## WHY IT PAYS TO BE JUST

One of Plato's objectives in the *Republic* was to show that justice is worthwhile—that just action is a good in itself, and that one ought to engage in just activity even when it doesn't seem to confer immediate advantage. Once he has completed his portrait of the most just man—the philosopher-king—he is in a position to fulfill this aim. In Book IX, Plato presents three arguments for the claim that it pays to be just. First, by sketching a psychological portrait of the tyrant, he attempts to prove that injustice takes such a wretched toll on a man's psyche that it could not possibly be worth it (whereas a just soul is untroubled and calm). Next, he argues that, though each of the three main character types (money-loving, honor-loving, and truth-loving) have their own conceptions of pleasure and of the corresponding good life (each choosing his own life as the most pleasant sort), only the philosopher is in the position to judge since only he is capable of experiencing all three types of pleasure. Finally, he tries to demonstrate that only philosophical pleasure is really pleasure at all; all other pleasure is only cessation from pain.

In all likelihood, Plato did not consider any of these to be the primary source of justice's worth. Plato's goal was to prove that justice is worthwhile *independent* of the advantages it confers, so for him to argue that the worth of justice lies in the enormous pleasure it produces is beside his point. To say that we should be just because it will make our life more pleasant, after all, is just to say that we should be just because it is to our advantage to do so. Instead, we should expect to find him arguing that the worth of justice lies in some other source, preferably having something to do with objective goodness. This is why many philosophers, from Plato's student Aristotle down to modern scholar Richard Kraut, believe that Plato's real argument for the worth of justice takes place long before Book IX. They think, plausibly, that Plato locates the worth of justice in justice's connection to the Forms, which he holds to be the most good things in the world. Justice is worthwhile, on this interpretation, not because of any advantage it confers, but because it involves grasping the Form of the Good and imitating it. The just man tries to imitate the Forms by making his own soul as orderly and harmonious as the Forms themselves.

# SUMMARY & ANALYSIS

## BOOK I

### SUMMARY

In the *Republic*, Plato, speaking through his teacher Socrates, sets out to answer two questions. What is justice? Why should we be just? Book I sets up these challenges. The interlocutors engage in a Socratic dialogue similar to that found in Plato's earlier works. While among a group of both friends and enemies, Socrates poses the question, "What is justice?" He proceeds to refute every suggestion offered, showing how each harbors hidden contradictions. Yet he offers no definition of his own, and the discussion ends in *aporia*—a deadlock, where no further progress is possible and the interlocutors feel less sure of their beliefs than they had at the start of the conversation. In Plato's early dialogues, *aporia* usually spells the end. The *Republic* moves beyond this deadlock. Nine more books follow, and Socrates develops a rich and complex theory of justice.

When Book I opens, Socrates is returning home from a religious festival with his young friend Glaucon, one of Plato's brothers. On the road, the three travelers are waylaid by Adeimantus, another brother of Plato, and the young nobleman Polemarchus, who convinces them to take a detour to his house. There they join Polemarchus' aging father Cephalus, and others. Socrates and the elderly man begin a discussion on the merits of old age. This discussion quickly turns to the subject of justice.

Cephalus, a rich, well-respected elder of the city, and host to the group, is the first to offer a definition of justice. Cephalus acts as spokesman for the Greek tradition. His definition of justice is an attempt to articulate the basic Hesiodic conception: that justice means living up to your legal obligations and being honest. Socrates defeats this formulation with a counterexample: returning a weapon to a madman. You owe the madman his weapon in some sense if it belongs to him legally, and yet this would be an unjust act, since it would jeopardize the lives of others. So it cannot be the case that justice is nothing more than honoring legal obligations and being honest.

At this point, Cephalus excuses himself to see to some sacrifices, and his son Polemarchus takes over the argument for him. He lays out a new definition of justice: justice means that you owe friends help, and you owe enemies harm. Though this definition may seem different from that suggested by Cephalus, they are closely related. They share the underlying imperative of rendering to each what is due and of giving to each what is appropriate. This imperative will also be the foundation of Socrates' principle of justice in the later books. Like his father's view, Polemarchus' take on justice represents a popular strand of thought—the attitude of the ambitious young politician—whereas Cephalus' definition represented the attitude of the established, old businessman.

Socrates reveals many inconsistencies in this view. He points out that, because our judgement concerning friends and enemies is fallible, this credo will lead us to harm the good and help the bad. We are not always friends with the most virtuous individuals, nor are our enemies always the scum of society. Socrates points out that there is some incoherence in the idea of harming people through justice.

All this serves as an introduction to Thrasymachus, the Sophist. We have seen, through Socrates' cross-examination of Polemarchus and Cephalus, that the popular thinking on justice is unsatisfactory. Thrasymachus shows us the nefarious result of this confusion: the Sophist's campaign to do away with justice, and all moral standards, entirely. Thrasymachus, breaking angrily into the discussion, declares that he has a better definition of justice to offer. Justice, he says, is nothing more than the advantage of the stronger. Though Thrasymachus claims that this is his definition, it is not really meant as a definition of justice as much as it is a delegitimization of justice. He is saying that it does not pay to be just. Just behavior works to the advantage of other people, not to the person who behaves justly. Thrasymachus assumes here that justice is the unnatural restraint on our natural desire to have more. Justice is a convention imposed on us, and it does not benefit us to adhere to it. The rational thing to do is ignore justice entirely.

The burden of the discussion has now shifted. At first, the only challenge was to define justice; now justice must be defined and proven to be worthwhile. Socrates has three arguments to employ against Thrasymachus' claim. First, he makes Thrasymachus admit that the view he is advancing promotes injustice as a virtue. In this view, life is seen as a continual competition to get more (more money, more power, etc.), and whoever is most successful in the competition has the greatest virtue. Socrates then launches into a long and complex chain of reasoning which leads him to conclude that injustice cannot be a virtue because it is contrary to wisdom, which is a virtue. Injustice is contrary to wisdom because the wise man, the man who is skilled in some art, never seeks to beat out those who possess the same art. The mathematician, for instance, is not in competition with other mathematicians.

Socrates then moves on to a new argument. Understanding justice now as the adherence to certain rules which enable a group to act in common, Socrates points out that in order to reach any of the goals Thrasymachus earlier praised as desirable one needs to be at least moderately just in the sense of adhering to this set of rules.

Finally, he argues that since it was agreed that justice is a virtue of the soul, and virtue of the soul means health of the soul, justice is desirable because it means health of the soul.

Thus ends Book I. Socrates and his interlocuters are no closer to a consensus on the definition of justice, and Socrates has only advanced weak arguments in favor of justice's worth. But the terms of our challenge are set. Popular, traditional thinking on justice is in shambles and we need to start fresh in order to defeat the creeping moral skepticism of the Sophists.

---

ANALYSIS

While the *Republic* is a book concerned with justice, it also addresses many other topics. Some scholars go so far as to say that the book is *primarily* about something other than justice. Critic Allan Bloom, for instance, reads the book first and foremost as a defense of philosophy—as Socrates' second "apology." Socrates was executed by the city of Athens for practicing philosophy. The leaders of Athens had decided that philosophy was dangerous and sought to expel it from their city. Socrates had called the old gods and the old laws into question. He challenged, and asked others to challenge, the fundamental beliefs upon which their society rested.

In the *Republic*, Bloom says, Plato is trying to defend the act for which his teacher was executed. His aim is to reveal why the philosopher is important, and what the philosopher's relationship to the city should be. While a philosopher is potentially subversive to any existing regimes, according to Plato, he is crucial to the life of the just city. Plato wanted to show how philosophy can be vital to the city. Bloom calls the *Republic* the first work of political science because it invents a political philosophy grounded in the idea of building a city on principles of reason.

Bloom's interpretation follows from an understanding of Plato's ideas about justice and just cities in the *Republic,* which is how the book demands to be read at first. Looking at the *Republic* as a work on justice, we first need to ask why justice has to be defended. As Thrasymachus makes clear, justice is not universally assumed to be beneficial. For as long as there has been ethical thought, there have been immoralists, people who think that it is better to look out for your own interest than to follow rules of right and wrong.

Traditionally, the Greek conception of justice came from poets like Hesiod, who in *Works and Days* presents justice as a certain set of acts that must be followed. The reason for being just, as presented by the traditional view, was consideration of reward and punishment: Zeus rewards those who are good and punishes those who are bad. In late fifth century Athens, this conception of divine reward and retribution had lost credibility. No one believed that the gods rewarded the just and punished the unjust. People could see that many unjust men flourished, and many of the just were left behind. In the sophisticated democracy that evolved in Athens, few were inclined to train their hopes on the afterlife. Justice became a matter of great controversy.

Leading the controversy were the Sophists, the general educators hired as tutors to the sons of the wealthy. The Sophists tended not to believe in objective truth, or objective standards of right and wrong. They regarded law and morality as conventions. The Sophist Antiphon, for example, openly declared that we ought to be unjust when being unjust is to our advantage.

Plato felt that he had to defend justice against these onslaughts. The Sophistic challenge is represented in the *Republic* by Thrasymachus, who declares that justice is nothing but the advantage of the stronger. Since this statement motivates the entire defense that is to follow, it deserves analysis. What exactly does Thrasymachus mean by claiming that justice is the advantage of the stronger? Who are the stronger? What is their advantage?

On the first reading, Thrasymachus' claim boils down to the basic Sophistic moral notion that the norms and mores we consider just are conventions that hamper those who adhere to them and benefit those who flout them. Those who behave unjustly naturally gain power and become rulers and strong people in society. When stupid, weak people behave in accordance with justice, they are disadvantaged, and the strong are at an advantage. An alternate reading of Thrasymachus' bold statement makes his claim seem more subtle. On this reading, put forward by C.D.C. Reeve, Thrasymachus is not merely making the usual assertion that the norms and mores of justice are conventions; he is further claiming that these mores and norms are conventions put in place by rulers to promote their own interests and to keep their subjects in a state of oppression.

This second reading is interesting because it challenges not only our conception of right and wrong, but Socrates' usual way of finding truth. Socrates' method of *elenchus* proceeds by building up knowledge out of people's true beliefs. If Thrasymachus is right, then we do not have any true beliefs about justice. All we have are beliefs forced on us by rulers. In order to discover the truth about right and wrong, we must abandon the old method and start from scratch: building up knowledge without resting on traditional beliefs. In the next book, Plato abandons the method of *elenchus*. and begins the discussion from scratch.

Regardless of how we interpret Thrasymachus' statement, the challenge to Socrates is the same: he must prove that justice is something good and desirable, that it is more than convention, that it is connected to objective standards of morality, and that it is in our interest to adhere to it.

# BOOK II

## SUMMARY: BOOK II, 357A–368C

Socrates believes he has adequately responded to Thrasymachus and is through with the discussion of justice, but the others are not satisfied with the conclusion they have reached. Glaucon, one of Socrates' young companions, explains what they would like him to do. Glaucon states that all goods can be divided into three classes: things that we desire only for their consequences, such as physical training and medical treatment; things that we desire only for their own sake, such as joy; and, the highest class, things we desire both for their own sake and for what we get from them, such as knowledge, sight, and health. What Glaucon and the rest would like Socrates to prove is that justice is not only desirable, but that it belongs to the highest class of desirable things: those desired both for their own sake and their consequences.

Glaucon points out that most people class justice among the first group. They view justice as a necessary evil, which we allow ourselves to suffer in order to avoid the greater evil that would befall us if we did away with it. Justice stems from human weakness and vulnerability. Since we can all suffer from each other's injustices, we make a social contract agreeing to be just to one another. We only suffer under the burden of justice because we know we would suffer worse without it. Justice is not something practiced for its own sake but something one engages in out of fear and weakness.

To emphasize his point, Glaucon appeals to a thought experiment. Invoking the legend of the ring of Gyges, he asks us to imagine that a just man is given a ring which makes him invisible. Once in possession of this ring, the man can act unjustly with no fear of reprisal. No one can deny, Glaucon claims, that even the most just man would behave unjustly if he had this ring. He would indulge all of his materialistic, power-hungry, and erotically lustful urges. This tale proves that people are only just because they are afraid of punishment for injustice. No one is just because justice is desirable in itself.

Glaucon ends his speech with an attempt to demonstrate that not only do people prefer to be unjust rather than just, but that it is rational for them to do so. The perfectly unjust life, he argues, is more pleasant than the perfectly just life. In making this claim, he draws two detailed portraits of the just and unjust man. The completely unjust man, who indulges all his urges, is honored and rewarded with wealth. The completely just man, on the other hand, is scorned and wretched.

His brother, Adeimantus, breaks in and bolsters Glaucon's arguments by claiming that no one praises justice for its own sake, but only for the rewards it allows you to reap in both this life and the afterlife. He reiterates Glaucon's request that Socrates show justice to be desirable in the absence of any external rewards: that justice is desirable for its own sake, like joy, health, and knowledge.

## ANALYSIS: BOOK II, 357A–368C

Coming on the heels of Thrasymachus' attack on justice in Book I, the points that Glaucon and Adeimantus raise—the social contract theory of justice and the idea of justice as a currency that buys rewards in the afterlife—bolster the challenge faced by Socrates to prove justice's worth. With several ideas of justice already discredited, why does Plato further complicate the problem before Socrates has the chance to outline his own ideas about justice?

The first reason is methodological: it is always best to make sure that the position you are attacking is the strongest one available to your opponent. Plato does not want the immoralist to be able to come back and say, "but justice is only a social contract" after he has carefully taken apart the claim that it is the advantage of the stronger. He wants to make sure that in defending justice, he dismantles all the best arguments of the immoralists.

The accumulation of further ideas about justice might be intended to demonstrate his new approach to philosophy. In the early dialogues, Socrates often argues with Sophists, but Thrasymachus is the last Sophist we ever see Socrates arguing with. From now on, we never see Socrates arguing with people who have profoundly wrong values. There is a departure from the techniques of *elenchus* and *aporia*, toward more constructive efforts at building up theory.

The *Republic* was written in a transitional phase in Plato's own life. He had just founded the Academy, his school where those interested in learning could retreat from public life and immerse themselves in the study of philosophy. In his life, Plato was abandoning Socrates' ideal of questioning every man in the street, and in his writing, he was abandoning the Sophist interlocuter and moving toward conversational partners who, like Glaucon and Adeimantus, are carefully chosen and prepared. In the dialogues, they are usually Socrates' own students.

Plato had decided at this point that philosophy can only proceed if it becomes a cooperative and constructive endeavor. That is why in his own life he founded the Academy and his writings paired Socrates with partners of like mind, eager to learn. Glaucon and Adeimantus repeat the challenge because they are taking over the mantle as conversational partners. Discussion with the Sophist Thrasymachus can only lead to *aporia*. But conversation with Glaucon and Adeimantus has the potential to lead to positive conclusions.

This might seem like a betrayal of his teacher's mission, but Plato probably had good reason for this radical shift. Confronting enemies has severe limits. If your viewpoint differs radically from that of your conversational partner, no real progress is possible. At most, you can undermine one another's views, but you can never build up a positive theory together.

## SUMMARY: BOOK II, 368D-END

> *The result, then, is that more plentiful and better-*
> *quality goods are more easily produced if each person*
> *does one thing for which he is naturally suited, does it at*
> *the right time, and is released from having to do any of*
> *the others.*

*(See* QUOTATIONS, *p. 75)*

Socrates is reluctant to respond to the challenge that justice is desirable in and of itself, but the others compel him. He lays out his plan of attack. There are two kinds of justice political—the justice belonging to a city or state—and individual—the justice of a particular man. Since a city is bigger than a man, he will proceed upon the assumption that it is easier to first look for justice at the political level and later inquire as to whether there is any analogous virtue to be found in the individual. To locate political justice, he will build up a perfectly just city from scratch, and see where and when justice enters it. This project will occupy the *Republic* until Book IV.

Socrates introduces the foundational principle of human society: the principle of specialization. The principle of specialization states that each person must perform the role for which he is naturally best suited and that he must not meddle in any other business. The carpenter must only builds things, the farmer must only farm. Behind this principle is the notion that human beings have natural inclinations that should be fulfilled. Specialization demands not only the division of labor, but the most appropriate such division. Only in this way, Socrates is convinced, can everything be done at the highest level possible.

Having isolated the foundational principle of the city, Socrates is ready to begin building it. The first roles to fill are those that will provide for the necessities of life, such as food, clothing, health, and shelter. The just city is populated by craftsmen, farmers, and doctors who each do their own job and refrain from engaging in any other role. They are all members of what Socrates deems the "producing class," because their role is to produce objects for use.

Socrates calls this city the "healthy city" because it is governed only by necessary desires. In the healthy city, there are only producers, and these producers only produce what is absolutely necessary for life. Glaucon looks less kindly on this city, calling it a "city of pigs." He points out that such a city is impossible: people have unnecessary desires as well as these necessary ones. They yearn for rich food, luxurious surroundings, and art.

The next stage is to transform this city into the luxurious city, or the "city with a fever." Once luxuries are in demand, positions like merchant, actor, poet, tutor, and beautician are created. All of this wealth will necessarily lead to wars, and so a class of warriors is needed to keep the peace within the city and to protect it from outside forces. The producers cannot act as our warriors because that would violate our principle of specialization.

Socrates spends the rest of this book, and most of the next, talking about the nature and education of these warriors, whom he calls "guardians." It is crucial that guardians develop the right balance between gentleness and toughness. They must not be thugs, nor can they be wimpy and ineffective. Members of this class must be carefully selected—people with the correct nature or innate psychology. In particular, guardians should be spirited, or honor-loving, philosophical, or knowledge-loving, and physically strong and fast.

Nature is not sufficient to produce guardians. Nature must be protected and augmented with education. The education of guardians will involve physical training for the body, and music and poetry for the soul. Education of guardians is the most important aspect of the city. It is the process of purification through which the unhealthy, luxurious city can be purged and purified. Because the education of the guardians is so important, Socrates walks us through it in painstaking detail.

He begins by describing what sort of stories will be permitted in the city. The stories told to the young guardians-in-training, he warns, must be closely supervised, because it is chiefly stories that shape a child's soul, just as the way parents handle an infant shapes his body. The remainder of Book II, therefore, is a discussion of permissible tales to tell about the gods. Socrates comes up with two laws to govern the telling of such stories. First, the gods must always be represented as wholly good and as responsible only for what is good in the world. If the gods are presented otherwise (as the warring, conniving, murderous characters that the traditional poetry depicts them to be), children will inevitably grow up believing that such behavior is permissible, even admirable. Second, the gods cannot be represented as sorcerers who change themselves into different forms or as liars. Otherwise, children will grow up without a proper reverence for truth and honesty.

## ANALYSIS: BOOK II, 368D-END

The basic principle of education, in Plato's conception, is that the soul, like the body, can have both a healthy and unhealthy state. As with the body, this state is determined by what the soul consumes and by what it does. Education determines what images and ideas the soul consumes and what activities the soul can and cannot engage in. Since the soul is always consuming, the stimuli available in the city must be rigidly controlled. Plato compares souls to sheep, constantly grazing. If you place sheep in a field of poisoned grass, and they consume this grass little by little, they will eventually sicken and die. Similarly, if you surround a soul with unwholesome influences, then gradually the soul will take these in and sicken. For this reason, Plato does not limit himself to dictating the specific coursework that will be given to the guardians, but also dictates what will be allowed into the cultural life of the city as a whole. The guardians, like all others, are constantly absorbing images. Practically speaking, there is little difference between the official school curriculum and the cultural life of the city in general.

Plato prescribes severe dictates concerning the cultural life of the city. He rules out all poetry, with the exception of hymns to the gods and eulogies for the famous, and places restraints on painting and architecture. Though Plato expresses regret at these aesthetic sacrifices, he feels they must be made for the sake of education, which transforms the unhealthy luxurious city into a pure and just city. How does it do this? The answer will not become clear until we understand what political justice is.

We might also ask at this point whether it is only the education of the guardians that is so important. If education determines whether a soul is sick or healthy, do we not care about the souls of the other members of society? The answer, probably, is that we do care about educating all souls, but since we are currently focusing on the good of the city, we are only interested in what will effect the city as a whole. Because of the way our city is set up, with the producing class excluded from political life, their education is not as important to the good of the city as the education of the guardians. Although education is important for everyone, the education of the producers, which would focus on development of skills apprioriate to specialized vocation, is not as relevant to the good of the city as a whole. When the discussion turns to questions of the individual, Socrates will identify one of the main goals of the city as the education of the entire populace as far as they can be educated.

# BOOK III

## SUMMARY: BOOK III, 386A–412B

Socrates continues to discuss the content of stories that can be told to the guardians, moving on to stories about heroes. The most important function of this class of stories is to immunize the young guardians against a fear of death. Heroes must never be presented as fearing death or as preferring slavery to death. Hades—the place of dead souls—must never be presented as a frightening place. Heroes must never be presented as lamenting famous men as if their dying were a bad thing. Heroes should never be shown engaging in violent laughter since violent emotions in one direction usually lead to violent emotions in the other. Like the gods, they must always be portrayed as honest.

Glaucon raises the question of stories about normal mortal men, but Socrates postpones the issue. What poets currently say about men, he points out, is that the unjust often succeed and the just are wretched. They praise the former as wise and declare that it is good to be unjust if one can get away with it. Since it is our current mission to disprove these claims, it is not yet our place to outlaw this sort of story. We must first prove that these claims are false and only then can we outlaw these stories because they represent untruths.

Socrates discusses the style of stories that will be allowed. He lays out the most appropriate meter, and wonders whether these stories ought to be in dramatic or in lyric form. From here, he moves on to the other arts, such as painting and architecture. In all of these—as in poetry—he forbids the artists to represent characters that are vicious, unrestrained, slavish, and graceless. Any characteristics besides those the guardians should emulate are excluded.

Socrates moves on to what might seem like a surprising topic in a discussion on education: the correct love between a boy and a man. Socrates considered such relationships a vital part of a boy's education. His main point here is to warn against allowing any actual sexual intercourse to contaminate these relationships. They should not involve an erotic element, he explains, only a pure sort of love.

Physical training of the guardians is the next topic. This training, he warns, should resemble the sort involved in training for war, rather than the sort that athletes engage in. He emphasizes how important it is to properly balance the music and poetry with physical training. Too much physical training will make the guardians savage, while too much music and poetry will make them soft.

Socrates prescribes the medical training that should be provided in the just city. Doctors should be trained to treat the healthy, who suffer from a single, curable ailment. They should not be trained to deal with the chronically ill. Those suffering from an incurable physical disease should be left to die naturally. Those suffering from an incurable mental disease should actively be put to death.

---

## ANALYSIS: BOOK III, 386A-412B

The passage on the love between a man and a boy raises the question, what does love have to do with education? Eros, or proper love, is the emotion that motivates us to ascend to the heights of knowledge. As we will see later, true knowledge does not attach itself to the observable world around us. True knowledge, instead, has as its object the realm of the Forms, the universal, eternal truths that only our mind can access. Although study allows us to make the intellectual leap toward this higher realm, eros provides the emotional motivation for studying. For Plato, all action must be motivated by some desire or emotion. The emotional motivation that sends us looking for the Forms, then, is erotic love. Eros is the bridge between the physical world and the intelligible, the motivation for the philosopher's quest.

According to Plato's dialogue the *Symposium*, erotic love spurs us toward knowledge in several steps. We first love the beauty of one physical body. From there, we go on to love two physical bodies. We next move on to the love of all physical beauty, and then to a love of traditions and institutions, to beautiful studies, and finally, to one supreme study, the knowledge of beauty itself. Once we have reached beauty itself, or the Form of Beauty, the journey is complete. We have acheived knowledge and become real philosophers. So the topic of erotic love is perfectly suited to a discussion of education. Erotic love is necessary in the education of the philosopher.

Plato forbids sexual intercourse to enter into these relationships. In the highest sort of love—which leads to knowledge of the Forms—the goal is to lead the beloved to knowledge of truth and goodness. What the lover desires, more than anything, is to improve the soul of the beloved. But this only explains why love should not focus primarily on physical pleasure, not why Plato forbid it.

Plato saw sexual intercourse as serving no useful end. Heterosexual intercourse must be tolerated because it is necessary for procreation, but homosexual intercourse, he believed, serves no end but the fulfillment of physical pleasure. Since homosexual intercourse is useless, it cannot be good or beautiful. Whatever is neither good nor beautiful should be avoided. Second, as Plato makes clear later in the *Republic*, the health of a man's soul is determined by the desires he aims to fulfill. A just soul is a soul that pursues the right desires. Desire for physical pleasure is not worth fulfilling. So though the good man, the philosophical man, might have physical desires directed at his young friend, it is crucial to his virtue that he not act on these; he must not try to satisfy his lust for physical pleasure. Instead, he must transmute that erotic desire into a longing for truth and goodness, and a longing to find this truth and goodness together with his beloved.

---

## SUMMARY: BOOK III, 412C-END

Now that Socrates has finished laying out the proper education for guardians, he introduces the third and final class of the just society: rulers. The group until now has been called guardians is split. The best from this group will be chosen out as rulers, and only they will now be termed "guardians," while the rest will remain as warriors and will be termed "auxiliaries," because their role is to aid rulers by carrying out and enforcing their decisions.

To ensure the right selection of rulers, all the young guardians in training are closely observed. They are made to go through various tests which are intended to determine which of them remain steadfast in their loyalty to the city. They are exposed to various fears and pleasures meant to tempt or frighten them out of their convictions. Those who do best in these tests will proceed on to higher forms of education that will prepare them to rule. The rest, destined to be warriors, will end their education where Socrates left off. The further education of rulers is not discussed until Book VII.

To ensure that there is never controversy over who should rule, Socrates suggests telling all citizens a useful fiction, usually termed "the myth of the metals." The myth contends that all citizens of the city were born out of the earth. This fiction persuades people to be patriotic. They have reason to swear loyalty to their particular plot of ground and their fellow citizens. That plot of ground is their mother, and their fellow citizens are their brothers and sisters. The myth holds that each citizen has a certain sort of metal mixed in with his soul. In the souls of those most fit to rule there is gold, in those suited to be auxiliaries there is silver, and in those suited to be producers there is either bronze or iron. The city must never be ruled by someone whose soul is mixed with the wrong metal; according to an oracle, the city will be ruined if that ever happens.

The people must be told that though for the most part iron and bronze people will produce iron and bronze children, silver people silver children, and gold people gold children, that is not always the case. It is critical to observe the next generation to discover their class of soul. Those who are born to producers but seem to have the nature of a guardian or an auxiliary will be whisked away and raised with other such children. Similarly, those born to guardians or auxiliaries who seem more fit as producers will be removed to that class of society. Although the just society is rigid in terms of adult mobility between classes, it is not as rigid in terms of heredity.

Plato ends the chapter with a brief discussion about housing provided for the guardians. The guardians, we are told, all live together in housing provided for them by the city. Guardians receive no wages and can hold no private wealth or property. They are supported entirely by the city through the taxation of the producing class. One last useful fiction that will be told to the guardians is that it is unlawful for them to even handle gold or silver—that it is impious for them to mix earthly gold and silver with the divine silver and gold in their souls. Socrates' reasoning is clear: if the rulers are permitted to acquire private property, they will inevitably abuse their power and begin to rule for their own gain, rather than the good of the entire city.

---

## ANALYSIS: BOOK III, 412C-END

Most first-time readers of the *Republic* are shocked by how authoritarian Plato's ideal city is. In this section, many of the authoritarian aspects come to the fore. Personal freedom is not valued. The good of the state overrides all other considerations. Social classes are rigid, and people are sorted into these classes with no thought to their preferences. Of course, Plato would object to this latter claim by saying that each person will find their class most pleasing to them since it is best suited to their nature. Nonetheless, they are given no input when the state determines what life they will lead. A citizen's fate—producer, warrior, or ruler—is decided at an early age, and no provisions are made for individuals to shift classes as they mature.

Those labelling the ideal city authoritan can also point to state-controlled propaganda in the form of the myth of the metals. The irony is that for someone who claimed to value truth so highly, Plato has little trouble justifying wide-scale deception. The good of the state overrides all else, including the importance of truth.

But rather than draw back from this authoritarian utopia in horror, we might do well to suspend judgement for the time being. As we read through the *Republic,* we should ask ourselves why we value personal freedom so highly and what we might be sacrificing by placing such a high priority on freedom.

# BOOK IV

### SUMMARY: BOOK IV, 419A-434C
Adeimantus interrupts Socrates to point out that being a ruler sounds unpleasant. Since the ruler has no private wealth, he can never take a trip, keep a mistress, or do the things that people think make them happy. Socrates responds by reminding his friends that their goal in building this city is not to make any one group happy at the expense of any other group, but to make the city as a whole as happy as it can be. We cannot provide the guardians with the sort of happiness that would make them something other than guardians. He compares this case to the building of a statue. The most beautiful color in the world, he states matter-of-factly, is purple. So if our intention were to make the statue's eyes as beautiful as possible, we would paint them purple. Since no human being actually has purple eyes this would detract from the beauty of the statue as a whole, so we do not paint the eyes purple. On the statue, as in the city, we must deal with each part appropriately, in order to make the situation best for the whole.

Socrates proceeds to address several topics regarding the lifestyle of the guardians. He tells the money-loving Adeimantus that there will be no wealth or poverty at all in the city since there will be no money. Adeimantus objects that a city without money cannot defend itself against invaders, but Socrates reminds Adeimantus that our city will have the best warriors and points out that any neighboring city would be happy to come to our aid if we promised them all the spoils of war. Socrates limits the size of the city, warning against it becoming so large that it can no longer be governed well under the current system. He suggests that guardians guard their own elementary education above all else, and that they share everything in common among them, including wives and children. He declares that the just city has no use for laws. If the education of guardians proceeds as planned, then guardians will be in a position to decide any points of policy that arise. Everything we think of as a matter of law can be left to the judgement of the properly educated rulers.

Socrates declares the just city complete. Since this city has been created to be the best city possible, we can be sure that it has all the virtues. In order to define these virtues, all we need to do is look into our city and identify them. So we will now look for each of the four virtues: wisdom, courage, moderation, and justice.

We find wisdom first. Wisdom lies with the guardians because of their knowledge of how the city should be run. If the guardians were not ruling, if it were a democracy, say, their virtue would not translate into the virtue of the city. But since they are in charge, their wisdom becomes the city's virtue. Courage lies with the auxiliaries. It is only their courage that counts as a virtue of the city because they are the ones who must fight for the city. A courageous farmer, or even ruler, would do the city no good. Moderation and justice, in contrast to wisdom and courage, are spread out over the whole city. Moderation is identified with the agreement over who should rule the city, and justice, finally, is its complement—the principle of specialization, the law that all do the job to which they are best suited.

So now we have reached one of our two aims, at least partially. We have identified justice on a city-wide level. Our next task is to see if there is an analogous virtue in the case of the individual.

### ANALYSIS: BOOK IV, 419A-434C

Socrates has at last provided a definition of justice. This definition bears strong resemblance to the two definitions of justice put forward in Book I. Cephalus ventured that justice was the honoring of legal obligations, while his son Polemarchus suggested that justice amounts to helping one's friends and harming one's enemies. These two definitions are linked by the imperative of rendering what is due, or giving to each what is appropriate. This same imperative finds variant expression in Plato's definition of justice—justice as a political arrangement in which each person plays the appropriate role. What is due to each person is rendered all at once. Each is assigned the role in society that best suits their nature and that best serves society as a whole.

In one sense, Polemarchus and Cephalus were not that far off the mark. However, in following the traditional notions, they were thinking about justice as a set of actions, rather than as a structure to society, a phenomenon that spreads out over a city as a whole.

In addition to the definition of justice, we also get the definitions of four other virtues in this section. The city's courage, Socrates tells us, is located in the auxiliaries, because it is only their courage that will effect the city as a whole. Yet right after making this claim, he goes on to tell us that what the auxiliaries possess is not simply courage but something he calls "civic courage." Many scholars have interpreted civic courage as a kind of second-rate courage. What the auxiliaries have, Socrates tells us, is the right beliefs about what is to be feared and what is not to be feared. Their courage is founded upon belief, rather than knowledge. Later in the book, he indicates that real virtue must be founded upon knowledge, suggesting that virtue based on habit or belief and not knowledge will fail when the going gets very tough. Since only the guardians possess knowledge, only the guardians can be truly virtuous or courageous.

---

## SUMMARY: BOOK IV, 435D-END

Now that Socrates has identified societal justice, he turns to look for individual justice. Justice in the individual, as in the city, involves the correct power relationship among parts, with each part occupying its appropriate role. In the individual, the "parts" are not classes of society; instead, they are aspects of the soul—or sources of desire.

In order to make the case that individual justice parallels political justice, Socrates must claim that there are precisely three parts of the soul. By cataloging the various human desires, he identifies a rational part of the soul that lusts after truth, a spirited part of the soul that lusts after honor, and an appetitive part of the soul that lusts after everything else, including food, drink, sex, and especially money. These three parts of the soul correspond to the three classes in the just city. The appetite, or money-loving part, is the aspect of the soul most prominent among the producing class; the spirit or honor-loving part is most prominent among the auxiliaries; and reason, or the knowledge-loving part, is dominant in the guardians.

Just relations between the three parts of the soul mirror just relations among the classes of society. In a just person the rational part of the soul rules the other parts, with the spirited part acting as helper to keep the appetitive in line. Compare this to the city where the truth-loving guardians rule, with the honor-loving auxiliaries acting as their helpers to keep the money-loving producers in line. What it means for one part of the soul to "rule" the others is for the entire soul to pursue the desires of that part. In a soul ruled by spirit, for instance, the entire soul aims at achieving honor. In a soul ruled by appetite, the entire soul aims at fulfilling these appetites, whether these be for food, drink, sex, fine material goods, or hordes of wealth. In a just soul, the soul is geared entirely toward fulfilling whatever knowledge-loving desires reason produces.

Socrates has now completely fulfilled his first goal: he has identified justice on both the political and individual levels. Yet in giving an account of justice, he has deviated from our intuitive notions of what this virtue is. We tend to think of justice as a set of actions, yet Socrates claims that justice is really a result of the structure of the soul. After identifying individual justice, he demonstrates that a person who's soul is in the right arrangement will behave according to the intuitive norms of justice. He needs to show that the notion of justice we have just arrived at is not counter to our intuitions—that this notion accounts for our intuitions and explains them. Socrates points out that since our just person is ruled by a love of truth, he will not be in the grips of lust, greed, or desire for honor. Because of this, Socrates claims, we can rest assured that he will never steal, betray friends or his city, commit adultery, disrespect his parents, violate an oath or agreement, neglect the gods, or commit any other acts commonly considered unjust. His strong love of truth weakens urges that might lead to vice.

Socrates concludes Book IV by asserting that justice amounts to the health of the soul: a just soul is a soul with its parts arranged appropriately, and is thus a healthy soul. An unjust soul, by contrast, is an unhealthy soul. Given this fact, we are now in a position to at least suspect that it pays to be just. After all, we already admitted that health is something desirable in itself, so if justice is the health of the soul then it too should be desirable. Plato feels that he is not ready just yet to make the argument in favor of justice's worth. He puts off the definitive proofs until Book IX.

## ANALYSIS: BOOK IV, 435D-END

The word justice is applied by Plato to both societies and individuals, and Plato's overall strategy in the *Republic* is to first explicate the primary notion of political justice, then to derive an analogous concept of individual justice. Plato defines political justice as being inherently structural. A society consists of three main classes of people—the producers, the auxiliaries, and the guardians. The just society consists in the right and fixed relationships between these three classes. Each of these groups must do the appropriate job, and only that job, and each must be in the right position of power and influence in relation to the other.

In this section, Plato sets out to show that the three classes of society have analogs in the soul of every individual. In other words, the soul, like the city, is a tripartite entity. The just individual can be defined in analogy with the just society; the three parts of his soul are fixed in the requisite relationships of power and influence. In order to make this claim work, Plato must prove that there really are three parts of the soul.

There are two distinct legs of the argument for the tripartite soul, and the relationship between them is obscure. The first leg attempts to establish the presence of three distinct sets of desire in every individual. The second leg argues that these three sets of desire correspond to three distinct sources of desire, three distinct parts of the soul. The ultimate conclusion is that every individual has a tripartite soul. Plato has to classify the desires, because setting out to prove that there are three distinct parts of the soul without first establishing that there are these three types of desire, would not be as stylistically effective or compelling. The first leg bridges the transition from the societal to the individual level by showing that group properties stem from individual properties.

Why is it important for Plato to demonstrate that the three types of desire present in every individual correspond to three independent sources of desire? Why would it not be sufficient to maintain that these three forces are manifested at different times by the same subject, but do not correspond to three distinct parts of the soul?

This distinction allows the three types of desire to be exerted simultaneously. Political justice is a structural property, consisting in the relationships of three necessary parts. The relationships constituting political harmony are fixed and static in the same sense as the mathematical ratios that constitute musical harmony. In the individual, though desires come and go, the relationship between the different sets of desires remains fixed. The three-part division of the soul is crucial to Plato's overall project of offering the same sort of explication of justice whether applied to societies or individuals.

Plato begins his argument for the tripartite soul by setting up a criterion for individuation. The same thing cannot be affected in two opposite ways at the same time (436C). As pairs of opposites, he includes "assent and dissent, wanting to have something and rejecting it, taking something and pushing it away" (437B). Plato argues for the truth of this claim by bringing analogies from the behavior of bodies—a method which may seem illegitimate, given that he wants to use the principle to apply to aspects of the soul (in particular, opposing desires), not to physical objects.

In order to make the leap from observations about forces and desires to conclusions about parts of the soul, Plato relies throughout the argument on a suppressed metaphysical claim. Where there is desire, there is the agent of desire: the thing which desires. Using this premise and the criterion for individuation, he will arrive at three distinct parts of the soul, corresponding to the three aspects he has identified within the city.

Plato first tries to establish the existence of a purely appetitive part of the soul using this method. Thirst is a desire. There is a subject of this desire. Thirst is a desire for unqualified drink—that is, no particular kind of drink, just drink (437E). Now comes a logical digression, the aim of which is to preclude the combination of appetitive and rational forces in the same subject. The outcome of the logical digression is that if the truth about A is relative to the truth about B, then if B is qualified in a certain way, A must be analogously qualified (438A-E). Therefore, the agent of thirst desires drink unqualified (439B).

Because the agent desires unqualified drink rather than good drink, healthful drink, etc., it cannot be argued that this subject is a combination of appetitive and rational forces. The subject corresponding to thirst is characterized by pure animal urge, with no rational discrimination. If, on the other hand, the desire for drink were theoretically inextricable from the desire for good or healthy drink, there would be no pure appetite, and correspondingly no purely appetitive subject.

The desire for drink is representative of a whole class of desires which stem from the same agent. Other appetitive desires include hunger and lust for sex. The subject which desires unqualified food, drink, and sex is the appetitive part (437C). Plato feels no need to establish that the same agent is responsible for these various, though obviously related, desires. No reason is demanded for the identification of agents of desire, only for their separation.

Plato next attempts to isolate the rational part of the soul. He says that if there is a desire which opposes the appetitive desire, there is another, separate agent of desire. He then makes the empirical claim that there are sometimes thirsty people who do not wish to drink (439C). Therefore, there is an agent which desires to drink, and another agent which desires not to drink.

Plato then makes another empirical claim—that desires opposing the appetites always come from rational thought (439D). He concludes that the second agent's desires come from rational thought. He now believes himself to have identified a purely appetitive and a purely rational subject.

Plato is not justified in asserting that reason always opposes appetite. It is fairly easy to conceive of a situation in which spirit, rather than reason, would oppose appetite. Plato does not need to make as strong a claim that only reason opposes appetite. Instead, he could give an example of an anti-appetitive desire which does, in fact, happen to come from reason—for instance, not wanting the drink because it is unhealthy. He could then conclude that there is an agent other than appetite and that this agent's desires come from rational thought. Adding the extra claim that all desires which oppose appetitive desires stem from reason, is unnecessary, false, and inconsistent with a later step in this argument which shows spirit opposing the appetite.

It would be more problematic if one could imagine a situation in which two appetites are opposed to one another. Plato would respond, however, that it is reason which tells us that two conflicting appetitive desires are mutually exclusive, forcing us to view them as opposing desires.

Having argued for the existence of two different parts of the soul—one appetitive and the other rational—Plato needs only to establish that there is a third, spirited part of the soul in order to complete the analogy with the city. Once again, he begins this project by establishing the existence of a third branch of desire, as well as an agent of that desire. Anger and indignation are desires. There is an agent of these desires. Next, he tries to prove that this third agent does not reduce to either of the two already established.

He first shows that spirit is not appetite. A man can feel angry at his appetites (440a). The third agent is not the same as the appetitive part. In contrast with the other potential identifications—i.e. reason with appetite, spirit with appetite—the only possible identification Plato contemplates between spirit and reason places spirit in the position of reason's henchman, carrying out the desires reason dictates. Plato, therefore, does not use the regular criterion of individuation to distinguish spirit from reason. Instead, he attempts to show that spirit cannot amount to the henchman of reason because it sometimes acts in reason's absence. Children and animals have the desires of the third agent without having the reasoning part of the soul (441B). Therefore, the third agent is not the rational part of the soul. Plato concludes that there are three separate parts of the soul: appetite, spirit, and reason.

In what way are these three distinct parts, and in what way do they make up a unified whole? Plato's argument for a tripartite soul in Book IV, as well as his description of the three parts of the soul in Book IX, depend primarily on identification of the soul and its parts through the desires exerted. Desires are active principles, forces that motivate the passive body. The soul, then, at least here, can be seen as a metaphysical entity which serves as the seat of human activity. The soul is the collection of active principles in a human being.

According to Plato, there are three main "psychological" forces at work in an individual—the force which has as its object physical entities and money; the force which has as its object nonmaterial but worldly entities such as honor and victory; and the force which has as its object the insensible realm of the Forms. These three forces are expressed in desires which correspond to appetite, spirit, and reason. All three of these forces make up one entity—the soul—in that they comprise the collective group of active principles in an individual. Yet they are distinct active principles which operate in different ways and have very different objects.

Because the soul is the seat of human forces, it is clear why Plato thought it appropriate to individuate its parts by demonstrating opposing desires within it. The best way to prove that there are independently working active forces within the soul is to demonstrate these forces exerting themselves in opposition to one another. Clearly the same active force cannot be responsible for the exertion of two opposing forces. Revealing opposing desires amounts to revealing discrete active forces within the collective seat of activity.

Plato uses this criterion of individuation to demonstrate that there are three active forces within the soul. While he does succeed in isolating three types of desire, he does nothing to prove that there are no more than three active forces. Perhaps rather than a tripartite soul, there is really a quadpartite or quinpartite soul. What evidence does Plato have to restrict it to three?

Plato's tripartite analysis of the soul puts forth at least three quite substantive claims. First, there are psychological agents of desire that possess the forces that act upon the body. Second, the multitudes of desires that an individual possesses can be reduced to three main categories, corresponding to three such psychological agents of desire that control human behavior. Third, the fundamental description of human psychology—that of the "structure of the soul"—has ethical implications and is necessary to an understanding of justice.

While the first and third claims have little currency among modern thinkers, the tripartite division of the individual psyche or soul has remained a viable hypothesis in accounting for internal psychological conflicts in the modern era. It survives, in modified forms, in such modern reincarnations as Freud's tripartite division between the id, the ego, and the superego.

# BOOK V

### SUMMARY: BOOK V, 449A-472A

Having identified the just city and the just soul, Socrates now wants to identify four other constitutions of city and soul, all of which are vicious to varying degrees. But before he can get anywhere in this project, Polemarchus and Adeimantus interrupt him. They would like him to return to the statement he made in passing about sharing spouses and children in common. Socrates launches into a lengthy discussion about the lifestyle of the guardians.

In the first of several radical claims that he makes in this section Socrates declares that females will be reared and trained alongside males, receiving the same education and taking on the same political roles. Though he acknowledges that in many respects men and women have different natures, he believes that in the relevant respect—the division among appetitive, spirited, and rational people—women fall along the same natural lines as men. Some are naturally appetitive, some naturally spirited, and some naturally rational. The ideal city will treat and make use of them as such.

Socrates then discusses the requirement that all spouses and children be held in common. For guardians, sexual intercourse will only take place during certain fixed times of year, designated as festivals. Males and females will be made husband and wife at these festivals for roughly the duration of sexual intercourse. The pairings will be determined by lot. Some of these people, those who are most admirable and thus whom we most wish to reproduce, might have up to four or five spouses in a single one of these festivals. All the children produced by these mating festivals will be taken from their parents and reared together, so that no one knows which children descend from which adults. At no other time in the year is sex permitted. If guardians have sex at an undesignated time and a child results, the understanding is that this child must be killed.

To avoid rampant unintentional incest, guardians must consider every child born between seven and ten months after their copulation as their own. These children, in turn, must consider that same group of adults as their parents, and each other as brothers and sisters. Sexual relations between these groups is forbidden.

Socrates explains that these rules of procreation are the only way to ensure a unified city. In most cities the citizens' loyalty is divided. They care about the good of the whole, but they care even more about their own family. In the just city, everyone is considered as family and treated as such. There are no divided loyalties. As Socrates puts it, everyone in the city says "mine" about the same things. The city is unified because it shares all its aims and concerns.

The final question to be asked is whether this is a plausible requirement—whether anyone can be asked to adhere to this lifestyle, with no family ties, no wealth, and no romantic interludes. But before answering this question, Socrates deals with a few other issues pertaining to the guardians' lifestyle, all of them relating to war. He states that children training to become guardians should be taken to war so they can watch and learn the art as any young apprentice does. He recommends that they be put on horseback so that they can escape in the case of defeat. He also explains that anyone who behaves cowardly in war will be stripped of their role as a guardian. He ends by discussing the appropriate manner in which to deal with defeated enemies. When it comes to Greek enemies, he orders that the vanquished not be enslaved and that their lands not be destroyed in any permanent way. This is because all Greeks are really brothers, and eventually there will be peace between them again. When it comes to barbarian—i.e., non-Greek—enemies, anything goes.

---

### ANALYSIS: BOOK V, 449A-472A

Plato advocates the equal education of women in Book V, but it would be inaccurate to think that Plato believed in the modern notion of equality between the sexes. He states in this section that women are inferior to men in all ways, including intellect. He could not have thought that all women were inferior to all men, or else dividing women into the three classes would make no sense. Instead, he believed that within each class the women are inferior to the men. So, for instance, guardian women would be superior to men of the two other classes, but inferior to most men of their own class.

With regard to the larger topic of family life, we might ask why common families are limited to the guardian class. Given that this arrangement is offered as a guarantee for patriotism, a preemptive strike against divided loyalties, why should it only apply to this class of society? The first thing to point out in relation to this topic is that the restrictions on family life are probably meant to apply to both the guardian and the auxiliary classes. These two classes are, after all, raised and educated together until adolescence when the rulers are chosen out as the best among the group, so chances are that their lifestyles are the same as well. Plato is often sloppy with the term "guardian," using it to apply sometimes only to the rulers and other times to both rulers and warriors. It is likely that the restriction on personal wealth also applies to auxiliaries.

The only class left out of this requirement is the producers. Since the producers have little to do with the political life of the city—they do not have to make any decisions pertaining to the city, or to fight on behalf of the city—their patriotism does not matter. Just as we saw that a courageous farmer does no good for the city as a whole, a patriotic craftsman or doctor is irrelevant from the standpoint of the society's good. The producers' only political task is to obey.

### SUMMARY: BOOK V, 471E-END

> *What about someone who believes in beautiful things*
> *but doesn't believe in the beautiful itself?*
> *(See* QUOTATIONS, *p. 75)*

Socrates has procrastinated long enough and must explain how guardians could be compelled to live in this bizarre way. His response is the most radical claim yet. Our system is only possible, he says, if the rulers are philosophers. Thus he introduces the concept of the philosopher-king, which dominates the rest of the *Republic*.

To back up this shocking claim, Socrates must explain, of course, what he means by the term "philosopher." Clearly he cannot mean to refer to the sort of people who are currently called "philosophers," since these people do not seem fit to rule. The first step in introducing the true philosopher is to distinguish these special people from a brand of psuedo-intellectuals whom Socrates refers to as the "lovers of sights and sounds." The lovers of sights and sounds are aesthetes, dilettantes, people who claim expertise in the particular subject of beauty.

In the distinction of the philosopher from the lover of sights and sounds the theory of Forms first enters the *Republic*. Plato does not explain through Socrates what the Forms are but assumes that his audience is familiar with the theory. Forms, we learn in other Platonic dialogues, are eternal, unchanging, universal absolute ideas, such as the Good, the Beautiful, and the Equal. Though Forms cannot be seen—but only grasped with the mind—they are responsible for making the things we sense around us into the sorts of things they are. Anything red we see, for instance, is only red because it participates in the Form of the Red; anything square is only square because it participates in the Form of the Square; anything beautiful is only beautiful because it participates in the Form of Beauty, and so on.

What makes philosophers different from lovers of sights and sounds is that they apprehend these Forms. The lovers of sights and sounds claim to know all about beautiful things but cannot claim to have any knowledge of the Form of the Beautiful—nor do they even recognize that there is such a thing. Because the lovers of sights and sounds do not deal with Forms, Socrates claims, but only with sensible particulars—that is, the particular things we sense around us— they can have opinions but never knowledge. Only philosophers can have knowledge, the objects of which are the Forms.

In order to back up this second radical claim—that only philosophers can have knowledge—Socrates paints a fascinating metaphysical and epistemological picture. He divides all of existence up into three classes: what is completely, what is in no way, and what both is and is not. What is completely, he tells us, is completely knowable; what is in no way is the object of ignorance; what both is and is not is the object of opinion or belief. The only things that are completely are the Forms. Only the Form of the Beautiful is completely beautiful, only the Form of Sweetness is completely sweet, and so on. Sensible particulars both are and are not. Even the sweetest apple is also mixed in with some sourness—or not-sweetness. Even the most beautiful woman is plain—or not-beautiful—when judged against certain standards. So we can only know about Forms, and not about sensible particulars. That is why only philosophers can have knowledge, because only they have access to the Forms.

ANALYSIS: BOOK V, 471E-END
In this section Plato makes one of the most important claims of the book: only the philosopher has knowledge. In fact, if we read the *Republic* as a defense of the activity of philosophy, as Allan Bloom

suggests, then this might be viewed as the most important claim. It explains why philosophy is crucial to the life of the city, rather than a threat to society.

The argument for this claim proceeds, roughly, as follows. Only "what is completely" is completely knowable. Only the Forms count as "what is completely." Only philosophers have access to the Forms. Only the philosophers have knowledge.

That only the Forms qualify as "what is completely" is a radical and contentious idea. Can a beautiful woman be completely beautiful? Is it not the case that she is only beautiful according to some standards, and not according to others? Compared to a goddess, for instance, she would probably appear plain. So the beautiful woman is not completely beautiful. No sensible particular can be completely anything—judged by some standards, or viewed in some way, it will lack that quality. It will certainly lose the quality over time. Nothing is sweet forever; fruit eventually withers, rots, dessicates. Nothing is beautiful forever; objects eventually corrode, age, or perish. The Form of Beauty is nothing but pure beauty that lasts without alteration forever. In Plato's conception, all Forms possess their singular qualities completely, eternally, and without change.

That only "what is completely" is completely knowable is a difficult idea to accept, even when we understand what Plato means to indicate by speaking of the Forms. Consider our beautiful woman. Remember that she is at the same time both beautiful and not beautiful and that her beauty must inevitably fade. So how can we know that she is beautiful, when she is not completely or permanently beautiful? To think that she is beautiful cannot amount to knowledge if it is partially false. But why can we not say that we know exactly in what way she is beautiful and in what ways not, that we know the whole picture? The reason that this does not work is that our beautiful woman is a changing entity, as are all sensible particulars. Since she herself is a changing entity, our grasp of her, if it is correct, has to change as well. Plato is adamant that knowledge does not change. Knowledge for Plato, as for Aristotle and many thinkers since, consists in eternal, unchanging, absolute truths, the kind that he would count as scientific. Since knowledge is limited to eternal, unchanging, absolute truths, it cannot apply to the ever changing details of the sensible world. It can only apply to what is completely—to what is stable and eternally unchanging.

Plato, some might claim, is making a mistake in leaping from the claim that knowledge must apply to stable, unchanging truths to the claim that knowledge only applies to Forms. His student Aristotle also believed that knowledge is limited to eternal and absolute truths, but he found a way to let knowledge apply to the world we observe around us by limiting knowledge to classes or kinds. We can have knowledge, in Aristotle's view, about human beings, but not about any particular human being. Classes, he realized, are stable and eternal, even if the particular entities that make them up are not.

In this section there are distinct echoes of earlier philosophers. In dividing all of existence up into three classes (what is completely, what is not at all, and what both is and is not), Plato draws on elements of pre-Socratic theories and synthesizes these elements into a coherent worldview. Parmenides is echoed in the extremes: in what is completely and in what is not at all. Parmenides spoke a great deal about "what is" and "what is not." He argued that all that exists— "what is"—is a single, unchanging, eternal thing—an entity that in many ways resembles the Forms (though it differs from the Forms, for instance, in that Parmenides' "what is" was a singular entity, while Plato allows for multiple Forms). Everything else, he said, is not at all. While Parmenides would have sympathized with Plato's two extremes, he would have strenuously objected to the existence of the middle realm—what both is and is not. By partaking of both "what is" and "what is not," this realm would have severely violated logic.

This realm, though, does have strong ties to another pre-Socratic philosopher, Heraclitus. One of Heraclitus' main doctrines was a theory concerning unity of opposites: the idea that whatever is beautiful is also ugly, whatever up also down, and so forth.

He believed that the entire world was composed out of these unities of opposites and that the key to understanding nature was to understand how these opposites cohered.

It is not surprising to find Plato drawing on these two thinkers, since he studied with students of both Parmenides and Heraclitus before he founded his Academy.

# Book VI

## Summary: Book VI, 484a–502c

> *Don't you think that the true captain will be called a*
> *real stargazer, a babbler, and a good-for-nothing by*
> *those who sail in ships governed in that way?*
> *(See* Quotations, *p. 76)*

Given that only philosophers can have knowledge, they are clearly the ones best able to grasp what is good for the city, and so are in the best position to know how to run and govern the city. If we only knew that they were virtuous—or at least not inferior to others in virtue—then, Socrates' friends agree, we could be sure that they are the ones most fit to rule. Luckily, we do know that philosophers are superior in virtue to everyone else. A philosopher loves truth more than anything else ("philosopher" means "lover of truth or wisdom"); his entire soul strives after truth. This means that the rational part of his soul must rule, which means that his soul is just.

Adeimantus remains unconvinced. None of the philosophers he has ever known have been like Socrates is describing. Most philosophers are useless, and those that are not useless tend to be vicious. Socrates, surprisingly, agrees with Adeimantus' condemnation of the contemporary philosopher, but he argues that the current crop of philosophers have not been raised in the right way. Men born with the philosophical nature—courageous, high-minded, quick learners, with faculties of memory—are quickly preyed upon by family and friends, who hope to benefit from their natural gifts. They are encouraged to enter politics in order to win money and power by their parasitic family and friends. So they are inevitably led away from the philosophical life. In place of the natural philosophers who are diverted away from philosophy and corrupted, other people who lack the right philosophical nature, rush in to fill the gap and become philosophers when they have no right to be. These people are vicious.

The few who are good philosophers (those whose natures were somehow not corrupted, either because they were in exile, lived in a small city, were in bad health, or by some other circumstance) are considered useless because society has become antithetical to correct ideals. He compares the situation to a ship on which the ship owner is hard of hearing, has poor vision, and lacks sea-faring skills.

All of the sailors on the ship quarrel over who should be captain, though they know nothing about navigation. In lieu of any skill, they make use of brute force and clever tricks to get the ship owner to choose them as captain. Whoever is successful at persuading the ship owner to choose him is called a "navigator," a "captain," and "one who knows ships." Anyone else is called "useless." These sailors have no idea that there is a craft of navigation, or any knowledge to master in order to steer ships. In this scenario, Socrates points out, the true captain—the man who knows the craft of navigation—would be called a useless stargazer. The current situation in Athens is analogous: no one has any idea that there is real knowledge to be had, a craft to living. Instead, everyone tries to get ahead by clever, often unjust, tricks. Those few good philosophers who turn their sights toward the Forms and truly know things are deemed useless.

All that we need to make our city possible, Socrates concludes, is one such philosopher-king—one person with the right nature who is educated in the right way and comes to grasp the Forms. This, he believes, is not all that impossible.

### ANALYSIS: BOOK VI, 484A-502C

Continuing with the defense of the philosopher, Plato asserts in this section that the philosopher is not only the sole possesor of knowledge, he is also the most virtuous of men. Plato indicates that the philosopher's association with the Forms determines his virtue. By associating with what is ordered and divine (i.e., the Forms), the philosopher himself becomes ordered and divine in his soul. He patterns his soul after the Form of the Good.

Plato also offers a more intuitive explanation for why the philosopher is virtuous. Since all of him strives toward truth, his other desires are weakened. He has no real drive toward money, honor, pleasure, and so on. In short, he has none of the drives that can lead to immoral behavior. He would never be motivated to steal, lie, boast, act slavishly, or anything else of this sort. His emotions and appetites no longer provide a strong impetus toward vice.

This description makes it sound as if the philosopher's soul is in a state of monopoly rather than a state of harmony. Instead of being ruled by reason, appetite and spirit are absent entirely. Elsewhere, however, Plato states that the just man does retain all three sets of desires in robust forms. Though he loves truth most of all, he also desires pleasure and honor to a lesser extent. It is not clear how to reconcile this with the above picture. Perhaps we can simply assume that Plato was using excessively strong language when he spoke about the philosopher as if he had no drives other than the drive toward truth. But if the philosopher does retain his love of honor, money, and pleasure to a certain degree, then what guarantee do we have that he will never behave viciously? The likely answer is this: even if the philosopher might sometimes have desires that could lead to vicious acts, because reason dominates the other parts of his soul, he rarely if ever acts on these desires.

Still, a question remains about the philosopher's virtue. Allan Bloom points out that it sounds as if the philosopher is virtuous in a very strange way. He behaves virtuously mainly out of his preoccupation with ideas, and not out of the motivations we typically think of as marking the virtuous man. He is courageous, says Bloom, because he is constantly preoccupied with the eternal Forms and as a result is oblivious to life. He is not courageous because he is obedient to the city's rules about what is fearful and what is not. He is moderate because he has an immoderate love of the truth, not because he restrains his desires. He is just in money matters because money plays only a small role in getting him what he wants, and so he cares little about it. We get no indication that he is just in money matters because he cares deeply about giving each person his due.

Taking off from this observation, Bloom divides virtue into two sorts—civic and intellectual—and argues that the philosophers only have the second kind. The civic virtues rise from the needs of the city; they are characteristics that aid in the goal of preserving the city and its inhabitants. The intellectual virtues stem from the needs of philosophy; they are characteristics that aid in gaining knowledge. Plato, he thinks, mistakenly (or perhaps deliberately) identifies these, so that he is able to claim that the philosopher is virtuous in the first sense, when he is only really virtuous in the second.

We might ask how important this mistake is, if it is really being made. If the philosopher is only virtuous in the second sense, but not the first, does that make him unfit to rule? It sounds as if it would. After all, if he lacks the civic virtues, then he lacks the virtues that help him act for the good of the city. Plato is safe from this objection. What virtues does the ruler really need? So long as he behaves in the virtuous way, what do we care about his motivation? If he is acting only out of his love for wisdom, rather than out of his love for the city, does that harm the city in any way? What makes the philosopher the ideal ruler are not his virtues, but his knowledge. So long as his moral character does not pose a positive threat to the good of the city, we should not concern ourselves with the source of his virtues.

---

### SUMMARY: BOOK VI, 502D–END

> *. . . in the intelligible realm it controls and provides truth and understanding, so that anyone who is to act sensibly in private or public must see it.*
>
> (See QUOTATIONS, *p. 76*)

Now Socrates turns to the final stage in the construction of the just city: the question of how to produce philosopher-kings.

He had mentioned in Book III that the guardians-in-training are subjected to many tests so that rulers are chosen from among them. One point of the test, he told us then, was to see who was most loyal to the city. Now we see that another major point of these tests is to determine who among them can tolerate the most important subject. The most important subject for a philosopher-king, it turns out, is the study of Form of the Good. It is in understanding the Form of the Good, in fact, that someone gains the highest level knowledge and thus becomes fit to be a philosopher king.

Socrates explains that the Form of the Good is not what is commonly held to be good. Some think that the highest good is pleasure, while the more sophisticated think that it is knowledge. In fact, it is neither of these, but Socrates cannot really say directly what it is. The best he can do is give an analogy—to say "what is the offspring of the good and most like it." This analogy is the first in a string of three famous and densely interrelated metaphors that will stretch into the next book—the sun, the line, and the cave. In the course of developing these three metaphors, Socrates explains who the philosopher is, while working out his metaphysics and epistemology.

The sun, Socrates tells us, is to the visible realm what the Good is to the intelligible realm (the realm of Forms) in three respects. First, while the sun is the source of light, and hence, visibility in the visible realm, the Good is the source of intelligibility. Second, the sun is responsible for giving us sight, because it is only by incorporation of sun-like stuff into it that the eye is enabled to see. Similarly, the Good gives us the capacity for knowledge. Finally, the sun is responsible for causing things to exist (to "come to be") in the visible realm. The sun regulates the seasons, it allows flowers to bloom, and it makes animals give birth. The Good, in turn, is responsible for the existence of Forms, for the "coming to be" in the intelligible realm.

The Form of the Good, Socrates says, is "beyond being"—it is the cause of all existence.

The Form of the Good is responsible for all knowledge, truth, and for the knowing mind. It is the cause of the existence of the Forms in the intelligible realm, and the source for all that is good and beautiful in the visible realm. It is not surprising, then, that it is the ultimate aim of knowledge.

Yet not until we hear the next analogy do we understand just how important this Form of the Good is to knowledge. The analogy of the line is meant to illustrate the ways of accessing the world, the four grades of knowledge and opinion available to us. Imagine, says Socrates, a line broken into four segments. The bottom two segments represent our access to the visible realm, while the top two represent our access to the intelligible.

The lowest grade of cognitive activity is imagination. A person in the state of imagination considers images and reflections the most real things in the world. In Book X, we will see that art belongs to this class as well. It is less clear what Plato means by imagination, but he provides many interpretations.

The next stage on the line is belief. Belief also looks toward the realm of the visible, but it makes contact with real things. A person in the stage of belief thinks that sensible particulars are the most real things in the world.

Further up the line, there are two grades of knowledge: thought, and understanding. Although thought deals in Forms, it uses sensible particulars as images to aid in its reasoning, as when geometers use a picture of a triangle to help them reason about triangularity. Thought also relies on hypotheses, or unproven assumptions. Understanding uses neither of these crutches. Understanding is a purely abstract science. The reasoning involved deals exclusively with Forms, working with an unhypothetical first principle, which is the Form of the Good.

To reach understanding, an individual using the crutches necessary to thought, works his way up with philosophical dialectic toward the Form of the Good. Once you reach the Form of the Good, you have hit on your first principle, a universal proposition which makes all unproven hypotheses unnecessary. You now understand the Form of the Good, and all the other Forms as well. In a flash, you have reached the highest stage of knowledge.

## ANALYSIS: BOOK VI, 502D-END

Plato claims to have no way to explain the Form of the Good directly, but there is good reason to believe that he had something in mind as the highest good. Many scholars have believed that the Good was supposed to be identical with the One. The One represents unity, and unity, in turn, is closely related to determinacy. The advantage of this reading is that it helps to explain the connection between intelligibility and reality. Undoubtedly, something is only a real, determinate thing because it is a unified thing, a One. If this characteristic really is the Good, then it makes sense that the Good is responsible for all of reality. Nothing could be real, could exist, without this characteristic. In support of this reading, there are various points in the *Republic* where Plato emphasizes the importance of unity in the soul and in the city, remarking that a city without unity is not a real city.

A more likely candidate for the Form of the Good is harmony. Though Plato does praise unity at several points in the *Republic*, he praises harmony, order, and balance even more. Harmony between the three classes of society makes for a healthy, just city, and harmony in the soul makes for a healthy, just soul. When speaking of the superiority of the Forms, he often appeals to their supreme order, and explains that they make the philosopher virtuous by inspiring the same order in his soul. The good of each thing might simply be its appropriate harmony, order, balance, or proportion. What harmony could mean as applied to the Forms, since the Forms have no separate parts to harmonize, is less than obvious. But since Plato could not be more clear in his view that the Forms are the most ordered things, he must think there is some way to harmonize them. It might be this confusion—an inability to understand how the Forms can have harmony or order—that keeps Plato from being able to define the Form of the Good.

In the metaphor of the line, the most difficult stage to understand is imagination. Because in Book IX Plato indicates that art belongs to this category, many have understood imagination to refer to a state of mind in which products of art are viewed as the most real things. This state of mind is not as far-fetched as it might seem. Imagine a person who acquires his sense of self and of the world around him from images he sees on television or in movies. (In Plato's time, the equivalent art forms would be epic poetry and tragic theater.) Such a person is not that difficult to imagine. You might even know someone like this.

Other scholars, though, have wondered whether Plato holds that art belongs to the category of imagination. There are other understandings of imagination that do not refer to art at all. On one such interpretation, imagination refers to a state in which our perceptions of the world are completely uncritical. In this state, we do not attempt to relate one perception to another. We see a reflection, and do not differentiate this from the object it is reflecting. Belief, then, would be the stage in which we correlate our perceptions, but fail to subject them to critical analysis. A related reading pegs imagination as a state in which we do not look for explanations, and belief as a state in which we do look for explanations but only in particular terms, rather than universal terms.

Thought and understanding are easier to pin down because Plato is more explicit about them. Thought is abstract reasoning that makes use of images and unproven assumptions. Geometry is the perfect example. In reasoning about triangularity, for example, geometers make use of diagrams of triangles. In order to prove theorems, they need to appeal to certain axioms that are taken as true without any attempt at proof. Understanding makes the axioms and hypotheses of thought unnecessary by seizing on a single universal proposition on which the entire body of knowledge can be based.

# BOOK VII

## SUMMARY: BOOK VII, 514A-521D

In Book VII, Socrates presents the most beautiful and famous metaphor in Western philosophy: the allegory of the cave. This metaphor is meant to illustrate the effects of education on the human soul. Education moves the philosopher through the stages on the divided line, and ultimately brings him to the Form of the Good.

Socrates describes a dark scene. A group of people have lived in a deep cave since birth, never seeing the light of day. These people are bound so that they cannot look to either side or behind them, but only straight ahead. Behind them is a fire, and behind the fire is a partial wall. On top of the wall are various statues, which are manipulated by another group of people, lying out of sight behind the partial wall. Because of the fire, the statues cast shadows across the wall that the prisoners are facing. The prisoners watch the stories that these shadows play out, and because these shadows are all they ever get to see, they believe them to be the most real things in the world. When they talk to one another about "men," "women," "trees," or "horses," they are referring to these shadows. These prisoners represent the lowest stage on the line—imagination.

A prisoner is freed from his bonds, and is forced to look at the fire and at the statues themselves. After an initial period of pain and confusion because of direct exposure of his eyes to the light of the fire, the prisoner realizes that what he sees now are things more real than the shadows he has always taken to be reality. He grasps how the fire and the statues together cause the shadows, which are copies of these more real things. He accepts the statues and fire as the most real things in the world. This stage in the cave represents belief. He has made contact with real things—the statues—but he is not aware that there are things of greater reality—a world beyond his cave.

Next, this prisoner is dragged out of the cave into the world above. At first, he is so dazzled by the light up there that he can only look at shadows, then at reflections, then finally at the real objects—real trees, flowers, houses and so on. He sees that these are even more real than the statues were, and that those were only copies of these. He has now reached the cognitive stage of thought. He has caught his first glimpse of the most real things, the Forms.

When the prisoner's eyes have fully adjusted to the brightness, he lifts his sight toward the heavens and looks at the sun. He understands that the sun is the cause of everything he sees around him—the light, his capacity for sight, the existence of flowers, trees, and other objects. The sun represents the Form of the Good, and the former prisoner has reached the stage of understanding.

The goal of education is to drag every man as far out of the cave as possible. Education should not aim at putting knowledge into the soul, but at turning the soul toward right desires. Continuing the analogy between mind and sight, Socrates explains that the vision of a clever, wicked man might be just as sharp as that of a philosopher. The problem lies in what he turns his sharp vision toward.

The overarching goal of the city is to educate those with the right natures, so that they can turn their minds sharply toward the Form of the Good. Once they have done this, they cannot remain contemplating the Form of the Good forever. They must return periodically into the cave and rule there. They need periodically to turn away from the Forms to return to the shadows to help other prisoners.

## ANALYSIS: BOOK VII, 514A–521D

It is important to realize, when reading the allegory of the cave and of the line, that Plato means to depict not only four ways of think-

ing, but four ways of life. To use an example, imagine that a person
in each of these stages were asked to say what courage is. The understanding of courage would differ widely from stage to stage.

Working with a possible interpretation of the imagination stage,
an individual's notion of courage in this stage would appeal to
images from culture. Such an individual might try to explain courage by saying something like, "Luke Skywalker seems really courageous, so that's courage." An individual possessed of beliefs would
also appeal to a particular example, but the example picked would
be drawn from real life. There might be mention of the Marines or
New York City firemen.

Someone at the stage of thought, in contrast, will try to give a definition of courage. Perhaps they will give the definition offered by
Socrates in Book IV: courage as the knowledge of what is to be
feared and what is not to be feared. What separates the person
speaking from thought from the person possessed of understanding
is that the person speaking from thought cannot inform his views
with knowledge of the Form of the Good. They are working with
unproven hypotheses rather than the true first principle. Even if
their definition is correct, it is left open to attack and objection
because their grasp of the relevant concepts stops at a certain point.
Speaking from understanding, someone giving a definition compre-
hends all the terms in the definition and can defend each one of them
based on the first principle, the Form of the Good.

Because the Form of the Good illuminates all understanding once it
is grasped, knowledge is holistic. You need to understand everything to
understand anything, and once you understanding anything you can
proceed to an understanding of everything. All the forms are connected, and are comprehended together in the following way: you
work your way up to the Form of the Good through thought until you
grasp the Form of Good. Then, everything is illuminated.

Since the stages in the cave are stages of life, it seems fair to say
that Plato thought that we must all proceed through the lower stages
in order to reach the higher stages. Everyone begins at the cognitive
level of imagination. We each begin our lives deep within the cave,
with our head and legs bound, and education is the struggle to move
as far out of the cave as possible. Not everyone can make it all the
way out, which is why some people are producers, some warriors,
and some philosopher-kings.

Given that the philosopher-kings have made it out of the cave, it
might seem unfair that they are then forced back in. This is the

SUMMARY & ANALYSIS

worry that Socrates' friends raise at the end of this section. Socrates has three lines of response to this concern. First, he reminds us again that our goal is not to make any one group especially happy, but rather to make the city as a whole as happy as possible. Second, he points out that the philosopher-kings are only able to enjoy the freedom above ground that they do because they were enabled by the education the city afforded them. They were molded to be philosopher-kings so that they could return to the cave and rule. They owe the city this form of gratitude and service. Finally, he adds that the philosophers will actually want to rule—in a backhanded way—because they will know that the city would be less just if they refrained from rule. Since they love the Forms, they will want to imitate the Forms by producing order and harmony in the city. They would be loathe to do anything that would subject the city to disorder and disharmony. Socrates ends by remarking that the reluctance of the philosopher to rule is one of his best qualifications for ruling. The only good ruler rules out of a sense of duty and obligation, rather than out of a desire for power and personal gain. The philosopher is the only type of person who could ever be in this position, because only he has subordinated lower drives toward honor and wealth to reason and the desire for truth.

### SUMMARY: BOOK VII, 521E–END

Now we know what distinguishes the philosopher-king from everyone else: he knows the Form of the Good, and so he has an understanding of everything. But it is left for Socrates to tell us how to produce this sort of man. He must explain what sort of supplementary education is added to the general education we read about in Books II and III, in order to make the guardians turn their souls toward ultimate truth and seek out the Form of the Good. The answer, it turns out, is simple: they must study mathematics and philosophical dialectic. These are the two subjects that draw the soul from the realm of becoming—the visible realm—to the realm of what is—the intelligible realm.

Of these two, mathematics is the preparation and dialectic the ultimate form of study. Dialectic leaves behind sense perceptions and uses only pure abstract reasoning to reach the Good itself. Dialectic eventually does away with hypotheses and proceeds to the first principle, which illuminates all knowledge. Though he is enamored of dialectic, Socrates recognizes that there is a great danger in it. Dialectic should never be taught to the wrong sort of people, or even to the right sort when they are too young. Someone who is not prepared for dialectic will "treat it as a game of contradiction." They will simply argue for the sake of arguing, and lose all sense of truth instead of proceeding toward it.

After discussing mathematics and dialectic Socrates launches into a detailed description of how to choose and train the philosopher-kings. The first step, of course, is to find the children with the right natures—those who are the most stable, courageous, and graceful, who are interested in the subjects and learn them easily, who have a good memory, love hard work, and generally display potential for virtue. From early childhood, the chosen children must be taught calculation, geometry, and all other mathematical subjects which will prepare them for dialectic. This learning should not be made compulsory but turned into play. Turning the exercises into play will ensure that the children learn their lessons better, since one always applies oneself better to what is not compulsory. Second, it will allow those most suited to mathematical study to display their enjoyment, since only those who enjoy it will apply themselves when the work is presented as noncompulsory. Then, for two or three years, they must focus exclusively on compulsory physical training; they cannot do anything else during this time because they are so exhausted.

All along, whoever is performing best in these activities is inscribed on a list, and when physical training is over those on the list are chosen to proceed. The rest become auxiliaries. The children are now twenty, and those who have been chosen to go on with philosophical training now must integrate all of the knowledge of their early traing into a coherent whole. Those who manage this task successfully have good dialectical natures and the others have weak dialectical natures. Those who are best at this task, therefore, and also at warfare and various other activities, are then chosen out from among the rest at their thirtieth year and tested again, this time to see who among them can give up their reliance on the senses and proceed to truth on thought alone. Those who do well in this test will study dialectic for five years; the others will become auxiliaries.

After five years of dialectic, the young philosophers must "go back into the cave" and be in charge of war and other offices suitable to young people to gain experience in political rule. Here too, they are tested to see which of them remains steadfast in his loyalty and wisdom. After 15 years of this, at the age of 50, whoever performs well in these practical matters must lift up his soul and grasp the Form of the Good. Now philosopher-kings, they must model themselves, the other citizens, and the city on the Form of the Good that they have grasped. Though each of them will spend most of his time on philosophy, when his turn comes they must engage in politics and rule for the city's sake. The other important task they are charged with is to educate the next generation of auxiliaries and guardians. When they die they are given the highest honors and worshipped as demi-gods in the city.

Now Socrates has finally completed describing the just city in every one of its aspects. He ends Book VII by explaining how we might actually go about instituting such a city. His shocking solution is go into an already existing city, banish everyone over ten years old and raise the children in the manner he has just outlined.

---

### ANALYSIS: BOOK VII, 521E–END

Plato's outline for the education of the philosopher-king may provide some insight into the education students received in the early days of the Academy. We know that mathematics was heavily emphasized at the Academy, and that, in fact, many of the subfields which Plato discusses here under the heading of "mathematics" could only have been learned at the Academy at that time. The mathematician Theaetetus and the mathematician and astronomer Eudoxus, both teachers at the Academy, were the only thinkers in the ancient world who understood these higher mathematical subjects well enough to transmit them to others. They were actually the only ones even working in some of these embryonic fields. In addition, there is some indication that Plato did not offer his students training in dialectic, since he believed that dialectic should not be taught to anyone under thirty.

Why did Plato put so much weight on mathematics? Mathematics draws us toward the intelligible realm because it is beyond the realm of sensible particulars. When we move beyond applied mathematics (e.g., beyond counting out particular objects, or tracing the astronomical patterns of the planets we see) and begin to contemplate numbers in themselves, and to examine their relations to other numbers, then we begin to move from the sensible realm to the intelligible. Numbers, like Forms, are truly existing, non-sensible entities that we can only access through abstract thought. Contemplating numbers and numerical relations, then, shows us that there is some truth above the sensible, and that this truth is higher than the sensible in that it explains and accounts for the sensible.

Mathematics, viewed in this way, was probably meant to play two roles in the education of the philosopher. First, it sets the students sights on truths above the sensible world. It indicates that there are such truths, and instills the desire to reach them. Second of all, by contemplating these truths the student cultivates his use of abstract reason and learns to stop relying on sensation to tell him about the world. Mathematics prepares the student to begin the final study of dialectic, in which he will eventually give up the images and unproven assumptions of mathematics and proceed entirely on the faculty of abstract thought which he has honed.

Plato puts little stock in human senses. The true philosopher must be trained to ignore his senses in his search for truth. He must rely on thought alone. The true philosopher probably makes no use of empirical investigation—that is, he does not observe the world in order to find truths. Plato is at odds with the typical scientific approach to knowledge, in which observation is the most important ingredient. Plato is also at odds with his most famous student, Aristotle, who himself was the first known proponent of the observational method of scientific investigation.

# Book VIII

## Summary

Now that Socrates has finished describing the just city, he returns to the interrupted task of describing the four unjust constitutions of city and man. In addition to the aristocracy that we have been discussing for the past six books, and the philosopher-king who microcosmically embodies and rules this government, Socrates identifies four other city-man pairs: there is a timocracy, and the honor-driven man who resembles and rules that sort of government; there is oligarchy, which resembles and is ruled by a man driven by his necessary appetites; there is democracy, which resembles and is ruled by a man driven by his unnecessary appetites; and there is tyranny, which resembles and is ruled by a man driven by his unlawful appetites. Each of these constitutions is worse than the other, with a tyranny being the most wretched form of government, and the tyrannical man the most wretched of men. Unfortunately, since our city is human and all human things inevitably degenerate, these four unjust constitutions are not presented as mere theoretical possibilities: they are presented as the inevitable stages of degeneration that the just city will pass through over time.

Because the rulers of the just city will rely on their fallible sense perception in choosing the next generation of rulers, they will inevitably make mistakes over time. Soon the wrong sort of people will occupy positions of power. These people will want to change things so that rulers can have private property and focus on wealth, while the good among the rulers will want to preserve the old order and focus on virtue. After some battling between these factions, the resulting constitution will be a compromise: a timocracy. To satisfy the bad faction, the rulers will distribute all the land and houses in the city as private property among themselves, and enslave the producers as serfs. They will focus all their energy on making war and guarding against the enslaved producers. The rulers will still be respected and the warring-ruling class will not take part in farming, manual labor, or other money-making ventures. They will eat communally and devote themselves to physical training and training for war. But they will be afraid to appoint wise people as rulers, choosing instead to be ruled by spirited but simple people who will be more inclined toward war than peace. Although they will desire money, the love of victory and honor will be predominant.

The corresponding man is a man ruled by spirit. Such a man, Socrates explains, is produced in this way: he is the son of an aristocratic man who encourages the rational part of his son's soul. But the son is influenced by a bad mother and servants, who pull him toward the love of money. He ends up in the middle, becoming a proud and honor-loving man.

Next, the timocracy degenerates into an oligarchy. As the love of money and wealth grows, the constitution will change so that ruling is based entirely on wealth. Whoever has wealth and property above a certain amount will be allowed to take part in ruling, and whoever has less than this will have no say in government. This city has five faults according to Socrates. First, it is ruled by people who are not fit to rule. Second, it is not one city but two: one city of rich people and one of poor. These two factions do not make up a single city because they are always plotting against one another, and do not have common aims. Third, this city cannot fight a war because in order to fight, the rulers would have to arm the people, but they are even more afraid of the people—who hate them—than of outsiders. Fourth, it has no principle of specialization. The rulers also have peripheral money-making occupations. This city is the first to allow the greatest evil: people who live in the city without belonging to any class or having any role; people who are not producers, warriors, or rulers. This group includes beggars and criminals. Socrates calls these people "drones" and divides them into two sorts: harmless and dangerous, or "stinging."

The corresponding man is a thrifty money-maker. He is a timocrat's son, and at first emulates him. But then some disgraceful and unfair mishap befalls his father. The son, traumatized and impoverished, turns greedily toward making money and slowly amasses property again. His reason and spirit become slaves to appetite, as his only drive becomes the desire to make more money. Reason can only reason about how to make more money, while spirit only values wealth and has as its sole ambition more wealth. This man has evil inclinations but these are held in check because he is careful about his wealth; he does not want to engage in activity that would threaten him with the loss of what he has managed to build up from scratch.

Next, the oligarchy declines into a democracy. The insatiable desire to attain more money leads to a practice of lending money at high interests. Many in the city are driven to utter poverty while a few thrive. The impoverished sit idly in the city hating those with wealth and plotting revolution. The rich, in turn, pretend not to notice the dissatisfied masses. Finally, agitated by the stinging drones, the poor revolt, killing some rich, and expelling the rest. They set up a new constitution in which everyone remaining has an equal share in ruling the city. They give out positions of power pretty much by lot, with no notice of who is most fit for what role. In this city the guiding priority is freedom. Everyone is free to say what they like and to arrange their life as they please. There is complete license. We, therefore, find the greatest variety of character traits in this city. What we do not find is any order or harmony. No one occupies the appropriate roles.

In order to describe the corresponding man, Socrates must explain the difference between necessary and unnecessary desires. Necessary desires are those we cannot train ourselves to overcome, the ones that indicate true human needs (e.g. the desire for enough sustenance to survive). Unnecessary desires are those which we can train ourselves to overcome (e.g., desire for luxurious items and a decadent lifestyle). The oligarchic man is ruled by his necessary desires, but his son, the democratic man, is soon overcome by unnecessary desires. Whereas the father was a miser who only wanted to hoard his money, the son comes to appreciate all the lavish pleasures that money can buy. Manipulated by bad associates, he abandons reverence and moderation and begins to regard anarchy as freedom, extravagance as magnificence, and shamelessness as courage. When he is older, though, some of his virtues return and he is sometimes pulled toward moderation. Yet he thinks all pleasures (those of moderation and of indulgence) are equal, and he yields to whichever one strikes his fancy at the moment. There is no order or necessity to his life.

In the last stage of degeneration, democracy, the most free city, descends into tyranny, the most enslaved. The insatiable desire for freedom causes the city to neglect the necessities of proper ruling. The drones stir up trouble again. In the democracy, this class is even fiercer than in the oligarchy because they usually end up becoming the dominant political figures. There are two other classes in the democracy other than the drones: there are those who are most naturally organized and so become wealthy, and then there are those who work with their hands and take little part in politics. The drones deceive both these other classes, inciting them against each other. They try to convince the poor that the rich are oligarchs, and they try to convince the rich that the poor are going to revolt. In their fear, the rich try to limit the freedoms of the poor and in so doing come to resemble oligarchs. In response, the poor revolt. The leader of this revolt—the drone who stirs up the people—becomes the tyrant when the poor people triumph. He kills all the good people for fear that they will supplant him, then enslaves everyone else so that he can steal from them to support his lavish and extravagant lifestyle. He also needs to constantly make war, to distract people from what he is doing. He must pander to the worst segments of society—the other drones—to make them his bodyguards.

Socrates ends Book VIII without giving us the portrait of the corresponding man. This long psychological portrait is saved for the next book.

---

### ANALYSIS

Plato's critique of democracy is insightful and thought-provoking. His description of democracy's single-minded pursuit of freedom at the expense of other goods, and of the sort of men who tend to gain power in such a system, should give us pause. We must take these criticisms seriously when considering just how we want to judge Plato's own system. Is the loss of personal freedom really beyond sacrifice? Or might we actually be better off giving up freedom to gain order and harmony in return? In either case, we now know what Plato would say to us when he saw our terror at giving up our

SUMMARY & ANALYSIS

sacred liberties: he would tell us that we only cling desperately to our personal freedoms because our soul is disordered and unhealthy, our priorities skewed. We shrink from the idea of living in Plato's *Republic* because we are driven by the wrong desires—by the desire for money, physical pleasure, and honor. He would add that if we were driven by the correct desires, the desire for truth, order, harmony, and the good of our society as a whole, we would be more open to adopting Plato's system of government.

Explaining why the just city must inevitably degenerate over time Plato appeals to a myth. He calculates a number which he calls the "human number" and explains that this number controls better and worse births. Since the rulers will not be perfectly aware of the mathematics involves in calculating this number, they will inevitably make mistakes and mate at the wrong time. The next generation will be inferior to the previous, and rulers will be lacking.

The human number is probably supposed to represent the human good, the Form of the Good as applied to human beings. The Forms and the laws of the universe are mathematical. Just as there are mathematical formulae that describe the movement of the planets and stars, there are also mathematical formulae that describe all the aspects of man. Plato recognizes that there is no one actual number in the case of man or of the cosmos that perfectly sums up all these formulae. He believes that all aspects of reality can be expressed mathematically, and that this mathematical expression of man, space, and time is at least one part of the absolute, transcendent reality of the Form of the Good.

# BOOK IX

### SUMMARY: BOOK IX, 571A-580A

> *Under the tyranny of erotic love he has permanently*
> *become while awake what he used to become*
> *occasionally while asleep.*
>
> *(See QUOTATIONS, p. 77)*

Book IX opens with a long and psychologically insightful description of the tyrannical man. The tyrannical man is a man ruled by his lawless desires. Lawless desires draw men toward all sorts of ghastly, shameless, criminal things. Socrates' examples of lawless desires are the desires to sleep with one's mother and to commit a foul murder. All of us have lawless desires, Socrates claims. The proof is that these desires occasionally come out at night, in our dreams, when the rational part of us is not on guard. But only the tyrannical man allows these desires to emerge in his waking hours.

The tyrannical man is the son of the democratic man. His father is not lawless, but he does indulge unnecessary desires. Just like the father, the son is exposed to drones, men with lawless desires. But whereas the father had his own oligarchic father's thriftiness to pull him toward the middle road of democracy, this son, brought up on the democratic ethos, moves further toward lawlessness. The father and entire household try to win him back, but the ultimate triumph of the lawless is inevitable. The winning move of the drones is to implant an strong erotic love in the son: this love itself acts as a drone, and incites him to all manner of lawlessness. It makes him frenzied and mad, and banishes all sense of shame and moderation.

This man now lives for feasts, revelries, luxuries, and girlfriends. He spends so much money that he soon runs through all he has and needs to begin borrowing. Then, when no one will lend him any more, he resorts to deceit and force. We see him running the whole gamut of typically unjust acts in his insatiable need to quench his erotic lusts. First, he tries to get money out of his parents in all sorts of awful ways, then he starts breaking into houses, robbing temples, and finally committing murders. He has become while awake what he used to be only while asleep; he is living a nightmare. Erotic love drives this nightmare, keeping him lost in complete anarchy and lawlessness. He will dare to do anything to keep feeding the desires that erotic love produces. Soon he cannot trust anyone, and has no friends. The most decent parts of his soul are enslaved to the most vicious part, and so his entire soul is full of disorder and regret and is least free to do what it really wants. He is continually poor and unsatisfied, and he lives in fear.

After this frightening image of the tyrannical life, everyone is ready to agree that no life could be more wretched. Socrates, however, disagrees; there is one sort of life even worse than this one. That is the life of a man who is not only a private tyrant, but who becomes an actual political tyrant. To make us see that this life is even worse, he asks us to imagine what would happen if this private tyrant, along with his entire family and all his slaves, were moved to a deserted island. Without the law to protect him from his mistreated slaves, would not the tyrant fear terribly for his life and the life of his family? And what if he were then surrounded by people who did not look kindly on those who abused their slaves? Would he not then be in even greater danger? But this is just what it is like to be an actual tyrant. The tyrant is in continual danger of being killed in revenge for all the crimes he committed against his subjects, whom he has made into slaves. He cannot leave his own house for fear of all his enemies. He becomes a captive and lives in terror. The real tyrant is also in a better position to indulge all his awful whims and to sink further into degeneracy.

The tyrant, who is also the most unjust man, is the least happy. The aristocrat, the most just man, is the most happy. So we were wrong in Book II to conclude the opposite. This is the first of our proofs that it pays to be just.

## ANALYSIS: BOOK IX, 571A-580A

In his lifetime, Plato had only ever seen tyrants driven by lust and greed. We might wonder if his diagnosis of the tyrannical psyche would have been the same if he had lived to see the totalitarian regimes of the twentieth century. His portrait of the tyrant is a brilliant and astute analysis of the Greek despot, but it seems less successful at capturing the psyche of a Hitler, a Stalin, or a Pol Pot. Were these men really driven by their appetites, or were they driven instead by reason gone horribly wrong? Plato never considers the possibility that reason itself can lead us toward evil, and perhaps he would try to maintain his position even in the face of recent history. He might argue that even in the case of these tyrants, the true driving force was a greed for money and power, and that reason, though playing a tremendous part in their deeds, was only instrumental reason, serving the ends of a nightmarish, lawless appetite. He might even be able to make a plausible case for this claim, pointing to the high honor and splendorous wealth these men achieved. Yet it is difficult to completely dismiss the suspicion that the real motivating force behind at least some of these regimes was a perverse idea and not an insatiable appetite.

## SUMMARY: BOOK IX, 580D–END

Socrates has just provided us with one compelling reason to believe that justice is worthwhile: he has shown how much happier the just man is than the unjust. Now he provides us with a second argument for the conclusion that the just life is the most pleasant. There are three sorts of people in the world, goes the argument: truth-loving, honor-loving, and profit-loving. Each one of these people takes the greatest pleasure in whatever it is they most value and thinks that the best life is the life that involves the most of this pleasure. Yet among these, only one of them can be proved to be right. Only the philosopher is in a position to make this judgement, because only he has actually experienced all three pleasures. So we ought to believe the philosopher when he says that the pleasure of truth-seeking is the greatest pleasure. If the philosopher is right, the pleasure one gets from having a just soul (i.e., a soul aiming at fulfilling reason's desires) is the best kind of pleasure. So, once again, we see that it does pay to be just.

The next argument also involves pleasures. Socrates argues that the pleasure of the philosopher is the only real pleasure. All other pleasures are actually relief from pain, not positive pleasure. Other pleasures are not real pleasures because other desires can never be completely satisfied. All we do is quench those yearnings temporarily, easing the pain of wanting. The philosophical desire can be completely fulfilled by grasping the Form of the Good.

Socrates now calculates that a king lives 729 times more pleasantly than a tyrant. This calculation is not supposed to be taken seriously, but is intended to emphasize that the just man is much happier than the unjust.

Finally, Socrates presents two refashioned portraits of the just and unjust man to replace the false portraits outlined in Book II. He asks us to envision that every human being with three animals inside of him: a multi-headed beast, a lion, and a human. If a man behaves unjustly, he tells us, then he is feeding the beast and the lion, making them strong, and starving and weakening the human being so that he gets dragged along wherever the others lead. He also fails to accustom the three parts to one another and leaves them as enemies. In the just person, the human has the most control. He takes care of the beast like a farm animal, feeding and domesticating the tame heads and preventing the savage ones from growing. He makes the lion his ally. The three parts are friends with each other. Socrates runs through various vices, such as licentiousness and cowardice, and shows how the three parts run amok to cause these vices.

Socrates declares that it is best for everyone to be ruled by divine reason, and while ideally such reason would be within oneself, the second best scenario is to have reason imposed from outside. This is the aim of having laws. The purpose of laws is not to harm people, as Thrasymachus claims, but to help them. Laws impose reason on those whose rational part is not strong enough to rule the soul.

## ANALYSIS: BOOK IX, 580D–END

Plato's stated goal was to show that justice is worthwhile *even in the absence of* the rewards it might confer. In Book IX he argues that justice pays precisely because of such advantages. It will make for the most pleasurable life. If this is his argument, then he is failing to live up to his promises.

In fact, Plato made his argument for the worth of justice long before this, in Book VII. The true worth of justice, on this reading, stems from the connection of justice to the source of all worth in the universe, the Forms. Since the Forms are the ultimate good, and justice involves seeking, grasping, and imitating these, justice too is good and the just life is worthwhile. This is the interpretation that Aristotle favored, and contemporary philosophers such as Richard Kraut have attempted to revive this reading. Kraut explains this notion of worth in the following terms. For Plato, what makes a human life good, and a human value worthwhile, is its connection to an absolute external good, this external good being the Forms. He compares this Platonic point of view to the Christian worldview in which God is the greatest good, and bringing God into one's life is what gives each life worth, and also to nineteenth century Romantic conceptions in which life only becomes worthwhile when it is not cut off from nature and the natural order. In all of these cases, the human good consists in relation to some higher, supreme good outside ourselves.

If knowledge of the form of the good is what makes the just life worthwhile, does anyone but the philosopher live a worthwhile life? If the Forms are the source of all worth and only the philosophers consort with the Forms, what can we say about everyone else? Do they have no chance at all to live a good life? Plato might respond to this question by stressing that any man can bring his soul toward the Forms to some extent by making sure that their soul is ordered and harmonious. In other words, by being just—by making sure that reason rules spirit and appetite—a man lives a worthwhile life even if he never grasps the Forms with his intellect.

# BOOK X

## SUMMARY

Socrates has now completed the main argument of the *Republic*; he has defined justice and shown it to be worthwhile. He turns back to the postponed question concerning poetry about human beings. In a surprising move, he banishes poets from the city. He has three reasons for regarding the poets as unwholesome and dangerous. First, they pretend to know all sorts of things, but they really know nothing at all. It is widely considered that they have knowledge of all that they write about, but, in fact, they do not. The things they deal with cannot be known: they are images, far removed from what is most real. By presenting scenes so far removed from the truth poets, pervert souls, turning them away from the most real toward the least.

Worse, the images the poets portray do not imitate the good part of the soul. The rational part of the soul is quiet, stable, and not easy to imitate or understand. Poets imitate the worst parts— the inclinations that make characters easily excitable and colorful. Poetry naturally appeals to the worst parts of souls and arouses, nourishes, and strengthens this base elements while diverting energy from the rational part.

Poetry corrupts even the best souls. It deceives us into sympathizing with those who grieve excessively, who lust inappropriately, who laugh at base things. It even goads us into feeling these base emotions vicariously. We think there is no shame in indulging these emotions because we are indulging them with respect to a fictional character and not with respect to our own lives. But the enjoyment we feel in indulging these emotions in other lives is transferred to our own life. Once these parts of ourselves have been nourished and strengthened in this way, they flourish in us when we are dealing with our own lives. Suddenly we have become the grotesque sorts of people we saw on stage or heard about in epic poetry.

Despite the clear dangers of poetry, Socrates regrets having to banish the poets. He feels the aesthetic sacrifice acutely, and says that he would be happy to allow them back into the city if anyone could present an argument in their defense.

Socrates then outlines a brief proof for the immortality of the soul. Basically, the proof is this: X can only be destroyed by what is bad for X. What is bad for the soul is injustice and other vices. But injustice and other vices obviously do not destroy the soul or tyrants and other such people would not be able to survive for long. So nothing can destroy the soul, and the soul is immortal.

Once Socrates has presented this proof, he is able to lay out his final argument in favor of justice. This argument, based on the myth of Er, appeals to the rewards which the just will receive in the afterlife. According to the myth, a warrior named Er is killed in battle, but does not really die. He is sent to heaven, and made to watch all that happens there so that he can return to earth and report what he

SUMMARY & ANALYSIS

saw. He observes an eschatalogical system which rewards virtue, particularly wisdom. For 1000 years, people are either rewarded in heaven or punished in hell for the sins or good deeds of their life. They are then brought together in a common area and made to choose their next life, either animal or human. The life that they choose will determine whether they are rewarded or punished in the next cycle. Only those who were philosophical while alive, including Odysseus who chooses to be reborn as a swan, catch on to the trick of how to choose just lives. Everyone else hurtles between happiness and misery with every cycle.

ANALYSIS

In Book X, Plato at last pits philosophy-based education in confrontation with traditional poetry-based education. Plato has justified philosophy and the philosopher and now he displays them in relation to their rivals—the people who are currently thought most wise and knowledgeable—the poets.

The myth, in appealing to reward and punishment, represents an argument based on motivations Plato earlier dismissed. Glaucon and Adeimantus had specifically asked him to praise justice without appealing to these factors. Why is he now doing exactly that?

Allen Bloom suggests that the inclusion of this myth is connected to the distinction between philosophical virtue and civic virtue. Philosophical virtue is the kind of virtue the philosopher possesses, and this kind of virtue differs from the virtue of the normal citizen. So far, says Bloom, Plato has only shown that philosophical virtue is worthy in itself. He has not shown that civic virtue is worthy. Since Glaucon and Adeimantus and countless others are not capable of philosophical virtue, he must provide them with some reason to pursue their own sort of virtue. With the contrast between philosophical and civic virtue in mind, Plato describes the thousand year cycles of reward and punishment that follow just and unjust lives.

Yet on our understanding of what makes any virtue worthwhile—its connection to the Forms—Plato has sufficiently demonstrated the worth of both sorts of virtue. Philosophical virtue might be more worthwhile because it not only imitates the Forms, but aims at and consorts with them, but civic virtue is worthwhile as well because it involves bringing the Forms into your life by instituting order and harmony in your soul. Bloom, though, also has another plausible hypothesis for why Plato included the myth of Er, and this one coheres well with our understanding of justice's worth. The myth of Er, Bloom explains, illustrates once again the necessity of philosophy. The civic virtues alone are not enough. Only the philosophers know how to choose the right new life, because only they understand the soul and understand what makes for a good life and a bad one. The others, who lack this understanding, sometimes choose right and sometimes wrong. They fluctuate back and forth between good lives and miserable ones. Since every soul is responsible for choosing his own life, every person must take full responsibility for being just or unjust. We willingly choose to be unjust because of our ignorance of what makes for a just or unjust soul. Ignorance, then, is the only true sin, and philosophy the only cure.

# IMPORTANT QUOTATIONS
## EXPLAINED

1.  The result, then, is that more plentiful and better-quality goods are more easily produced if each person does one thing for which he is naturally suited, does it at the right time, and is released from having to do any of the others.

In Book II, Socrates introduces the principle of specialization. According to Plato, political justice boils down to this guiding rule—that everyone do that to which their nature best suits them, and not meddle in any other business. Producers must produce according to their natures (e.g., the farmer farms, the carpenter builds wooden objects, the artist paints, and the doctor heals); warriors must fight; and the philosophers must rule.

2.  What about someone who believes in beautiful things but doesn't believe in the beautiful itself and isn't able to follow anyone who could lead him to the knowledge of it? Don't you think he is living in a dream rather than a wakened state? Isn't this dreaming: whether asleep or awake, to think that a likeness is not a likeness but rather the thing itself that it is like?

In Book V, Socrates explains what distinguishes the lover of sights and sounds, the pseudo-intellectual, from the true philosopher. The lover of sights and sounds takes the sensible objects around him for the most real things, not recognizing that there is a higher level of reality in the intelligible realm. In particular, he goes around talking about beauty, billing himself as an expert on beauty, and yet he does not even realize that there is such a thing as the Form of the Beautiful, which is the cause of all sensible beauty.

3.     They don't understand that a true captain must pay
       attention to the seasons of the year, the sky, the stars, the
       winds, and all that pertains to his craft, if he's really to be the
       ruler of a ship. And they don't believe that there is any craft
       that would enable him to determine how he should steer the
       ship, whether the others want him to or not, or any
       possibility of mastering this alleged craft or of practicing it
       at the same time as the craft of navigation. Don't you think
       that the true captain will be called a real stargazer, a babbler,
       and a good-for-nothing by those who sail in ships governed
       in that way?

After Socrates presents his notion of a philosopher-king in Book VI,
Adeimantus objects by pointing out that all real-life philosophers
are either vicious or useless. Socrates responds by drawing an analogy
to a ship governed by violent men, ignorant of navigation. His intention is to demonstrate that a good philosopher would necessarily be
considered useless under current circumstances. True knowledge is not
valued in modern Athens, nor even believed possible, and so anyone
who tries to live their life by pursuing and praising real knowledge (as
the true philosopher must do) will be thought a useless fool.

4.     Once one has seen it, however, one must conclude that it is
       the cause of all that is correct and beautiful in anything, that
       it produces both light and its source in the visible realm, and
       that in the intelligible realm it controls and provides truth
       and understanding, so that anyone who is to act sensibly in
       private or public must see it.

Socrates describes the Form of the Good in Book VI, the ultimate
object of knowledge. The Form of the Good is the source of all other
Forms—the source of the entire intelligible realm, of intelligibility
itself, and of our cognitive capacity to know. Though Socrates is not
able to describe the Form of the Good explicitly, he attempts to give
us a sense of it by comparing it to the sun. It is only when a man
grasps the Form of the Good that he achieves the highest level of
cognition, understanding. When a guardian takes this last step he is
finally ready to become a philosopher-king.

5.  Under the tyranny of erotic love he has permanently become while awake what he used to become occasionally while asleep.

In Book IX, Socrates presents a long and psychologically astute portrait of the tyrannical man. The tyrannical man is governed by lawless desires, the sort of desires that in normal people only emerge occasionally in dreams (desires for illicit sexual unions or heinous murders). Leading him down this nightmarish path, and egging him constantly on to greater excess, is the tyrannical man's erotic lusts. Socrates deems erotic love the greatest tyrant of all, and regards it as a dangerous emotion, best avoided by good men.

# KEY FACTS

FULL TITLE
Republic

AUTHOR
Plato

PHILOSOPHICAL MOVEMENT
Plato was his own philosophical movement, known
as "Platonism."

LANGUAGE
Ancient Greek

TIME AND PLACE WRITTEN
Plato wrote the Republic in Athens around 380 B.C.

SPEAKER
As in nearly all of Plato's works, Socrates acts as
Plato's mouthpiece.

AREAS OF PHILOSOPHY COVERED
Though the Republic is primarily concerned with defining and
defending justice, it is in no way limited to ethics and political
philosophy. It also presents bold and fascinating theories in the
fields of epistemology and metaphysics.

PHILOSOPHICAL MOVEMENTS OPPOSED
Plato's main opposition in the Republic is the Sophists.

OTHER WORKS BY PLATO ON SIMILAR TOPICS
For more on Plato's political theory see the Laws. For
more on his theory of Forms see the Meno, the Phaedo,
and the Symposium.

# STUDY QUESTIONS & ESSAY TOPICS

## STUDY QUESTIONS

1.  *Why does Glaucon mention the myth of the Ring of Gyges? What intuition of ours is he trying to jog?*

In Book II, Glaucon tries to reinforce the challenge to justice that Socrates must meet in the remainder of the book. He argues that justice is the sort of good that is only desired for its consequences, not for its own sake. Justice, he claims, is a necessary evil that human beings endure out of fear and weakness. Because we can all suffer from one another's injustices, he explains, we agree, as a society, to behave justly and thus avoid greater harm. Given the chance to escape reprisals, though, any human being would choose to be unjust rather than just.

In order to illustrate this point, Glaucon appeals to the Ring of Gyges. According to mythology, this ring has the special power to make its possessor invisible. Glaucon's intention in invoking this magical entity is to argue that even the most just man only behaves as he does because of fear of reprisal. If such a man were able to behave unjustly with impunity—as he could if he were invisible—then he would do so.

Glaucon himself does not believe that justice is a necessary evil; he thinks that it is the highest form of good, the sort that is desired both for its own sake and for its consequences. His wish is that Socrates provide a compelling argument to this effect.

2.    *Why does Plato go to such lengths to prove that there
      are three distinct parts to the human soul? Explain both
      why he needs three aspects to the soul, and also why
      these aspects need to be distinct and independent from
      one another.*

Plato applies the word 'justice' to both societies and individuals,
and his overall strategy in the *Republic* is to first explicate the primary notion of political justice, and then to derive an analogous
concept of individual justice. Plato defines political justice as being
inherently structural. A society consists of three main classes of people—the producers, the auxiliaries, and the guardians; the just society consists in the right and fixed relationships between these three
classes. Each of these groups must do the job appropriate to it, and
only that job, and each must be in the right position of power and
influence in relation to the others.

   In Book IV, Plato demonstrates that these three classes of society
have analogs in the soul of every individual. The soul is a tripartite
entity. The just individual can be defined in analogy with the just
society; the three parts of his soul are fixed in the requisite relationships of power and influence.

   That is why Plato needs to show that there are three parts of the
soul, but we can still ask why it is important for Plato to demonstrate that the three types of desire present in every individual correspond to three independent sources of desire.

   This distinction of parts allows the three types of desire to be
exerted simultaneously and to coexist with each other in both con-
flict and harmony. Political justice is a structural property, consisting in the realization of required relationships between three classes.
The relationships constituting political harmony are fixed and static
in the same sense as are the mathematical ratios constituting musical
harmony. So in the just individual as well, though desires come and
go, the relationship between the different sets of desires remains
fixed and permanent.

3.    *Why does Plato banish the poets from his city?*

After defining justice and proving its worth, Socrates turns his criti-cal eye toward the poets. In a shocking move, he banishes nearly all poetry from his city (the only exceptions he makes are for hymns to gods and eulogies for famous men). Plato regrets this edict, feeling that it is an aesthetic sacrifice, but one necessitated by the greater good of the city; the poets, he feels, are too dangerous. He lays out three distinct, though related reasons for his harsh judgement.

His first gripe with the poets is that they deal in the least real things. Their wares are images, shadows, reflections. The objects of their art are, as Socrates puts it, far removed from "what is." By "what is," we understand the Forms—the unchanging, absolutes of the intelligible realm. The imperfect mutable copies of the Forms, sensible particulars such as trees, chairs, tables, flowers, are once removed from this most real realm. But the products of poetry are nothing but copies of these once-removed objects. Worse, since only the Forms can be objects of knowledge, the poets know nothing, though they are widely believed to have vast stores of knowledge.

In addition, poets make a practice of imitating the worst aspects of souls. They do not imitate the rational part, since this aspect is both hard to imitate and hard to understand. Instead, they imitate the appetitive part of the soul, and attempt primarily to gratify the appetites with laughter and cheap thrills.

Worst of all, poetry corrupts the soul, strengthening the appeti-tive part and weakening the rational. It encourages us to indulge in emotions like pity, amusement at base jokes, sympathy with sexual lusts. Because we feel these emotions vicariously through fictional characters, and not ourselves, we believe that we are safe. However, we do not realize that once we begin to allow these sorts of emotion reign they gain power and flourish. Soon we are feeling pity for our-selves, amusement at base events in our own life, and our own sex-ual lusts. Our appetitive part begins to gain control of the rational, and we are made unjust.

# SUGGESTED ESSAY TOPICS

1.  *Thrasymachus declares that justice is nothing but "the advantage of the stronger." What do you think he means? Make sure your interpretation of the statement explains how it serves as the challenge which the* REPUBLIC *sets out to meet.*

2.  *Why does Plato think that the guardians should share all of their goods in common? Is this the same reason that he thinks they should share spouses and children in common, or is there a different reason for this?*

3.  *According to Plato, what makes the philosopher-king the best possible ruler? Do you agree with his analysis?*

4.  *What is the allegory of the cave meant to illustrate? Explain how it does so. What primary conclusion are we meant to draw from this extended analogy?*

5.  *Plato's just city goes through three stages of development: trace these stages and explain why each is necessary. In which of these three stages does justice reside? Why?*

6.  *What is Plato's opinion of erotic love? Of the five character types that he describes in detail, with whom is erotic desire most closely associated? Relate this to his discussion of sexual activity in Book III.*

7.  *Why do you think Plato ends the* REPUBLIC *by invoking the myth of Er?*

# Review & Resources

## Quiz

1. What is Plato's aim in the *Republic*?

   A. To define justice
   B. To prove that justice is worthwhile to pursue for its own sake
   C. To prove that justice is the advantage of the stronger?
   D. To define justice and to prove that it is worthwhile to pursue for its own sake

2. Which of Socrates' interlocuters asserts that justice is nothing but the advantage of the stronger

   A. Adeimantus
   B. Thrasymachus
   C. Glaucon
   D. Polemarchus

3. Which of the following terms best describes Thrasymachus?

   A. Platonist
   B. Pre-Socratic
   C. Sophist
   D. Politician

4. What advantage does the Ring of Gyges confer on its wearers?

   A. It makes them invisible
   B. It makes them invincible
   C. It makes them maximally just
   D. It makes everything they touch turn to gold

5.  According to Glaucon, to which of the following classes do the majority of people relegate justice?

    A.  Goods that are only desired for their own sake
    B.  Goods that are only desired for their consequences
    C.  Goods that are desired both for their own sake and for their consequences
    D.  Goods that are not desired at all

6.  According to Socrates what is the fundamental principle on which all human society should be based?

    A.  The principle of specialization
    B.  From each according to his ability, to each according to his need
    C.  Moderation
    D.  Love of honor

7.  Which of the following is not a term applied to the first city Socrates describes?

    A.  Healthy city
    B.  Luxurious city
    C.  City of pigs
    D.  City of necessary desires

8.  Which of the following classes of society populates the first city?

    A.  Producers
    B.  Auxiliaries
    C.  Philosopher-kings
    D.  All of the above

9.  Which of the following is not considered an important aspect of the warriors' education?

    A.  Poetry
    B.  Music
    C.  Physical training
    D.  Dialectic

10. What is the aim of the warriors' education?

    A. To make them maximally fierce
    B. To make them maximally philosophical
    C. To make them maximally honor-loving
    D. To strike the delicate balance between brutishness and gentle qualities

11. Which of the following is not considered an aspect of the soul by Plato?

    A. The appetitive part
    B. The spirited part
    C. The rational part
    D. The emotive part

12. Which of the following statements is false?

    A. Justice on the individual level precisely parallels justice on the societal level
    B. In a just individual the entire soul is one big rational part
    C. The guiding principle behind justice is harmony
    D. In a just individual the entire soul aims at fulfilling the desires of the rational part

13. Which of the following is not a characteristic that marks the lifestyle of the guardians?

    A. They own no private property
    B. They only mate several times a year
    C. They are celibate
    D. They do not know which children are their own

14. What is the main purpose in propagating the myth of the metals among the citizens of the just city?

    A. To ensure that they all agree on who should rule
    B. To ensure that the rulers do not seek wealth
    C. To ensure that all citizens view one another as relatives
    D. To ensure that the warriors would rather die than allow their city to fall into enemy hands

15. What is the role of women in the city?

    A.   They are limited to the producing class
    B.   They belong to their own class of society
    C.   The role of women is never mentioned in the *Republic*
    D.   Women occupy all of the same roles that men occupy

16. What distinguishes the lover of sights and sounds from the philosopher?

    A.   He does not recognize the forms?
    B.   He is concerned only with beauty and not with the good
    C.   Though he recognizes that there are forms, he cannot manage to connect these to what he sees around him in the sensible world
    D.   He fails to recognize that everything that is beautiful is also ugly

17. According to Socrates, what is the ultimate subject of study for the philosopher-kings?

    A.   Mathematics
    B.   Dialectic
    C.   The Form of the Good
    D.   The Form of the Beautiful

18. To which of the following does Socrates compare the Form of the Good?

    A.   A line
    B.   The sun
    C.   A cave
    D.   A fire

19. According to Socrates, what is the lowest grade of cognitive activity?

    A.   Imagination
    B.   Belief
    C.   Thought
    D.   Confusion

20. What is the difference between thought and understanding

   A. Understanding makes use of images and hypotheses as crutches, whereas thought does not
   B. Understanding reasons about Forms whereas thought does not
   C. Thought makes use of images and hypotheses as crutches, whereas understanding does not
   D. Thought reasons about Forms whereas understanding does not

21. What does Socrates mean to illustrate with the allegory of the cave?

   A. The effects of education on the soul
   B. The effects of the intelligible realm on the soul
   C. The effects of the visible realm on the soul
   D. The stages of moral development through which a philosopher king must pass

22. At what age does a guardian finally become a philosopher-king, provided that he passes through all of the various tests?

   A. 30
   B. 40
   C. 50
   D. 60

23. Why is the philosopher king most fit to rule the city?

   A. Because only he has knowledge
   B. Because he is the most just of all
   C. Because only he does not want to rule
   D. All of the above

REVIEW & RESOURCES

24.   Which of the following statements best approximates
      Socrates' attitude toward democracy?

    A.   It is the most ideal form of government in theory, but
      can never work in practice
    B.   It is the ideal form of government and should be
      instituted
    C.   It is an anarchic and disordered form of government,
      second only to tyranny in its wretchedness
    D.   It is the most wretched form of government

25.   How do we know that the philosopher's pleasure is the
      greatest possible pleasure?

    A.   Because only he is in a position to judge and he says so
    B.   Because this coheres with our theory of justice
    C.   Because if it weren't, then it would not be worthwhile
      to be just and we know that it is
    D.   Because of the myth of Er

**ANSWER KEY:**

1: D; 2: B; 3: C; 4: A; 5: B; 6: A; 7: B; 8: A; 9: D; 10: D; 11:
D; 12: B; 13: C; 14: C; 15: D; 16: A; 17: C; 18: B; 19: A; 20:
C; 21: A; 22: C; 23: D; 24: C; 25: A

# SUGGESTIONS FOR FURTHER READING

BLOOM, ALLEN. "Interpretive Essay." *Republic*. New York: Harper
Collins Publishers, 1968.

REEVE, C.D.C. "Introduction." *Republic*. Indianapolis: Hackett
Publishing Company, 1992.

GRUBE, G.M.A. *Plato's Thought*. Indianapolis: Hackett Publishing
Company, 1980.

KRAUT, RICHARD. *The Cambridge Companion to Plato*.
Cambridge: Cambridge University Press, 1997.

REVIEW & RESOURCES